TRANSFORM YOUR TRAJECTORY

ERIC PFEIFFER

ENDORSEMENTS

"If you care deeply about personal development and empowering your life, this book is a must-have. Through a collection of timely personal stories and experiences, the reader is given unbelievable tools which allow us to make choices and ultimately gain back control."

Nick Jensen
Capitol Food Company
VP of Sales

"We all seek to better ourselves in some form or fashion. If you consider yourself to have a growth mindset, this book is for you. Eric's ability to teach how seemingly ordinary moments of our lives can be significantly transformative is a gift that he willingly shares with others. Tired of life seemingly happening to you instead of for you? Take a look inside."

Landry Fields
Atlanta Hawks
GM

"My company has benefitted enormously from Eric's guidance. After working with him, I've observed an increase in staff unity that has positively impacted every aspect of the business. This book reflects the best of Eric's teachings in an easy-to-follow text that anyone can access. Your team will thank you for reading his book."

John Levi
Capitol Food Company

"*Transform Your Trajectory* by Eric Pfeiffer is an enlightening book that explores the concept of Kairos moments and their profound influence on our life's path. Pfeiffer skillfully blends insightful anecdotes, practical wisdom, and transformative tools like the Kairos Circle, empowering readers to recognize and embrace pivotal moments, take personal responsibility, and chart a course towards personal growth and fulfillment. This book serves as an invaluable guide for those seeking to harness the power of these transformative moments and create a purpose-driven life."

NICK RESSLER
Atlanta Hawks & Ares Management Company

"In Eric Pfeiffer's newest must-read book, *Transform Your Trajectory*, he lays out a solid framework for living one's life more fully integrated and alive. He is vulnerable with his own journey and shows the reader through this lens how the tools he teaches in this book will change and enhance the experience of walking through life's opportunities. Eric's combination of transparent process and his tool kit sets the stage for anyone who is ready for positive change."

BOB HASSON
CEO HPCI
Co-host of *Exploring the Marketplace* podcast with Shawn Bolz; Author of *Shortcuts*, *Wired to Hear*, and *Business of Honor*

Copyright (C) 2023 Eric Pfeiffer

All rights reserved:

This book is protected under the copyright laws of the United States of America. No portion of this book may be reproduced, stored in a retrieval system, or transmitted in any form or by any means- electronic, mechanical, photocopy, recording, scanning or other- except for brief quotations in critical reviews or articles, without prior written permission of the author.

Requests for permission to make copies of any part of this work should be made to: MPWRcoaching.com

ISBN: 978-1-7373414-2-0 (PB)
ISBN: 978-1-7373414-3-7 (eBook)

Printed in the United States of America

Published by Gravitas House

www.gravitashouse.com

Edited by Suzanne Lathrop
Interior design and art by Olivier Darbonville
Cover design by Olivier Darbonville

TRANSFORM YOUR TRAJECTORY

How to Turn Your Most Challenging Moments
Into Life-Changing Breakthroughs

ERIC PFEIFFER

CONTENTS

DEDICATION		8
ACKNOWLEDGEMENTS		11

PART 1 – SIGNPOSTS

1	A WAKE UP CALL	15
2	SEIZING OUR MOMENTS	35
3	KAIROS MOMENTS	51

PART 2 – THE KAIROS CIRCLE

4	IDENTIFYING YOUR KAIROS MOMENTS	67
5	OBSERVE: Excavating Your Facts and Feelings	75
6	INTERPRET: Filtering for Significance and Insights	83
7	DISCOVER: Extracting Learning and Takeaways	97
8	PLAN: Developing Concrete and Calendarized Ways Forward	107
9	PARTNER: Inviting Support and Challenge to Stay the Course	121
10	PRACTICE: Measuring Your Progress by Reviewing What You're Doing	129
11	TRAJECTORY SHIFT = TRANSFORMATION	141

PART 3 – KEY APPLICATIONS OF THE KAIROS CIRCLE

12	SELF-COACHING	159
13	COACHING OTHERS	163
14	COLLABORATIVE DECISION-MAKING	167
15	CONFLICT ENGAGEMENT	171
16	REVIEWING PEOPLE & PROJECTS	183

AFTERWORD	187
APPENDIX: KAIROS TEMPLATES	191

To the two people whose shoulders I largely stand upon:

MY WIFE & MOST TRUSTED PARTNER –

I fell in love the first time I saw her. I knew she was powerful before I ever heard her speak a word or do anything. Just her presence was enough to shift the atmosphere in any room. Yes, she is gorgeous and yet, her inner qualities far outshone her outer ones.

With Kandi's permission, I share in this book one of the more difficult parts of our journey together over these 22 years. There have been many high and low moments along the way, but we hold onto the truth, "Anything worth doing is worth doing poorly until you get better." I did not know how to be married well, as it was not modeled for me, but with Kandi's compassionate perseverance she has given me permission to be on a journey of becoming a better husband, father and partner. For this, I owe her the world.

She has fought with me and for me, always with the intent of growth and transformation. I am in many ways who I am because of her willingness to stay engaged, encourage me, challenge me and never let me settle for less than what she sees in me.

POPS –

This book is also dedicated to the man who believed in me enough to let me marry his daughter. It was a huge risk, and one I'm sure he often questioned. Our relationship began as in-laws, but soon grew into friendship. Early on, I recognized he was the kind of man I wanted to emulate. He was full of integrity, authenticity and a stubborn work ethic. In the early days, I traveled by motorcycle 140 miles each week just to spend a few hours with him, sipping coffee and absorbing every bit of wisdom I could squeeze from our lengthy conversations.

Over the years, he respected my journey, careful never to tell me what to do, but always ready with counsel when asked. We saw each other through many challenges, waded through many disagreements, and still managed to enjoy spending countless hours together. Not everyone is as fortunate to have such a father-in-law. Today, I call him "Pops," a nod to his fatherly investment in my life for over 20 years, and an honor that falls well short of what he deserves.

He has been one of my fiercest advocates, my confidant (yes, even when I complained about marriage) and a mentor. He successfully ran a major national electric company for over 20 years but considers it no small responsibility to run the books for my company. Humility oozes from his every pore. He truly believes helping others succeed is his greatest success.

I love you both. My success is your success.

I dedicate this book to these beautiful people, who for so many years, loved me by creating space to process and learn from life events. They recognized that life is always happening, but the meaning, significance and purpose of life are discovered when we pause long enough to extract the learning available. That's what this book is about—pausing to extract the significance and purpose from our life experiences.

ACKNOWLEDGEMENTS

I am truly grateful to all those who, in small and large ways, contributed to the development and execution of this book.

First, to the amazing people who have been the primary context in which I stumble and fumble into my own growth, my family. Kandi, Charity, and Justus, I love you more than words can portray. Thank you for your patience, kindness, and endurance as I continue to become a better version of myself for everyone's sake. My life and leadership are a testimony to your partnership.

A big thank you to the MPWR Coaching Team, who have supported and cheered my efforts to develop content that will continually move the needle in the area of leadership performance.

I'd like to thank Suzanne Lathrop and her team for their dedication and resilience in this project. Their support and feedback was priceless and gave me courage to stay the course.

I would be remiss if I did not recognize all of the brilliant women and men who have gone before me in developing an understanding of how people operate best under pressure. The content of this book simply stands upon their shoulders, attempting to reach further.

PART ONE

SIGNPOSTS

01

A WAKE UP CALL

"Eric, I want a separation."

I couldn't believe the words spilling from my wife's mouth. I stared intently back at her, wondering if I had heard her correctly. My heart began racing and my mind whirled with shock. Did I hear her correctly? Did she really just tell me she wants a separation? This seemed so extreme. I remember being flooded with a potent cocktail of emotions, vacillating between utter surprise and anger. After so many years of marriage, raising children, and fighting through so many battles, how could she just want to throw it all away?

"Are you serious?" was all I could mutter.

She looked at me intently, with a kind of fierce sorrow in her eyes. "Eric, I don't know what else to do. I can't keep going like this any longer. It's not ok for me to let you continue treating our family the way you have. I have to set some boundaries for mine and the kid's sake."

I stared at the floor, her words playing over and over in my mind. What was happening? Was this the end? Was she leaving me? What would our kids think? What would our friends say? Kandi and I had mentored so many other couples through difficult times, and here we were on the brink of divorce?

WTF!

I had heard other friends talk about having out-of-body experiences in times of crisis, but nothing could have prepared me for the terrifying and perplexing sensations coursing through my body, mind and soul.

Under the immense pressure, my mind grasped for some strategy to make things better, to talk her off the edge. I searched deeply for the right words, but nothing. Deep inside, I knew there was no quick-fix, no protestation or rationale that would dig me out of this hole. But I tried. I dialed up old, familiar friends in the form of self-justification and projection to find an escape route.

I thought to myself: *Eric, maybe she's just being dramatic…*

Maybe she's just had a tough week.

Maybe this whole episode isn't about you at all.

Maybe this is about her own struggles with work and life.

Maybe you're just the scapegoat for her own problems.

Maybe she's blowing this whole thing out of proportion.

But as many times as I rehearsed these voices in my mind, I knew they wouldn't serve me well.

There were no excuses or apologies that could undo what had been done. For someone who uses words for a living, I felt completely incapacitated. I had nothing. I was stuck and feeling increasingly hopeless.

We had committed early in our marriage to not using "divorce" or "separation" as idle threats to one-up each other in arguments. So, I knew this was serious. Actually, it was more than serious. To declare her want of a separation meant she had no other recourse. She was at her wit's end. She was desperate. She had hit her breaking point. Certainly, over many years, we'd had our fair share of fights, disagreements and challenges, negotiating our different value systems and personalities. She had before mentioned separation in a couple of conversations, but never actually pulled the trigger. But this moment was different. Her words were more than an idle threat. She had had enough. She was dead serious.

I continued staring at the floor. Time stood painfully still. Neither of us spoke for a long time.

I knew deep inside we could not walk this one back. She was not looking for excuses or explanations. She had heard them all before. There we were, at a precipice. The next step felt like I would fall from a thousand-foot cliff. *Is my marriage over?* I couldn't believe it. The longer I stewed in my own thoughts, the more I felt like I was in a washing machine, tumbling, drowning, desperate for salvation.

How did we even get here? How did it all get so bad?

I desperately wished we could just rewind to a time when things weren't so intense, where we could figure it out and find a better path forward. But there was no rewind button. I knew we had passed a point of no return and she wasn't backing down from her position.

It was like waking up to a real nightmare of someone breaking into your home to rob your most valued possessions and you're moving in slow motion, powerless to do anything. You can't think clearly or respond. It's just happening, and you feel so incredibly helpless.

WAKE UP CALL

Looking back on this moment, I can say I've experienced plenty of these wake-up calls throughout my life. Sometimes, it's not until the pain of my current situation gets bad enough that I'm willing to own it, take responsibility, and fight for change. I'm not proud of this, but it's true. And every time I have one of these shocking wake-up calls, I come to realize there were so many signposts I had passed by on my way to the cliff's edge.

It was the learning that comes from many failed attempts at doing life well that prepared me for what I experienced next.

The oddest thing began to happen as I sat, silent before my wife. In the midst of desperation, anger, frustration, shock and despair, a subtle feeling began to emerge. At first, I had a hard time identifying what it was. It didn't seem to fit, but there it was anyway. I felt some relief.

That's right, I felt relief.

Only now can I make sense of it. Sitting with her words, the longer I resisted defending myself or projecting blame on Kandi, the more I felt relief well up inside me. Initially, I thought it was relief at the idea of being out of a marriage I was clearly failing in. But that wasn't it. I realized the feeling of relief was actually my soul taking its first breath in a long time.

Deep inside, I knew things weren't going well. I knew our marriage was struggling and dangerously close to an ultimatum. But I was so desperate to hold everything together. I was living in denial, blind to the signposts.

I understand now that my wife's words were only exposing a deeper longing inside me. Yes, it was painful; but also incredibly relieving. Why? Because somewhere deep inside of me, I was also desperately unhappy with who I was in this season.

> **Sometimes, we discover desperation is the motivating force we need to wake up to our life when all else fails.**

Sometimes, we discover desperation is the motivating force we need to wake up to our life when all else fails.

The relief I experienced was not from being let off the hook, but exactly the opposite. I felt relief being called out, to be seen for better and worse. We tend to avoid these types of exposures, but they are the sunlight we need to disinfect our internal ailments. Kandi's words were not a judgment of who I was, but a plea for something better. Her challenge was actually an invitation to wake up and pay attention to where my life was heading. Even though I had brought us to the edge of the cliff, I knew she wasn't giving up on me. She was fighting for me. She was fighting for us.

I wish I could say it was in this moment I had an epiphany, but it would be days of trudging through turbulent emotions and dark thoughts, before I finally invited some trusted people to help me process my situation. Thankfully, they loved me enough to speak hard truths and push me to my limits. Often, it's not until we reach the end of ourselves that we discover new possibilities. Taking a hard look at ourselves can be the most difficult thing we do; but it's also the bravest.

Taking a hard look at ourselves can be the most difficult thing we do; **but it's also the bravest.**

After many days, I embraced my predicament and requested another conversation with Kandi. I would do my best to take full responsibility for myself and the impact on our lives. I would acknowledge that I needed time to do deep work, where I could become a better version of myself. With all my strength, I clung to something a mentor had shared with me: *Nothing in your life will change until you change yourself first.*

We met. I remember taking a few deep breaths, looking up at my wife, and saying, "Babe, I get it. I understand. I would likely coach anyone in your position to do the same, to set a strong boundary, even separation. I have not been operating well. Frankly,

I don't like who I've been over the past year; how I've behaved in our marriage and in our home is unacceptable. And I've not been able to hear you. I need help. I take full responsibility for what you're sharing with me. I want to change."

She responded with, "I hope so." She wasn't being cynical, but operating from tentative optimism. We've learned after many years in marriage that talk is cheap. We hold ourselves and each other to the accountability of "proof in the pudding." I would need to go on a journey that would reveal practical changes in my behavior over an extended period of time before trust in this area could be rebuilt.

Let's be clear: no one likes to be exposed in this way. No one likes to find out they're operating poorly, failing, or falling short. Author Henry Cloud famously said, "We change our behavior when the pain of staying the same is greater than the pain of changing." Consequences give us the pain that motivates us to change." The relief I felt was that my eyes were being opened to the pain I was in and how my pain was affecting those I loved most. Fear of separation was the consequence that compelled me to do something. I had coped with my pain long enough, and finally, I believed the pain of staying the same was truly worse than whatever pain I might endure in pursuit of personal transformation.

I was incredibly grateful for an opportunity to heal myself and my marriage, but there was a looming question begging for my attention. How had it gotten so bad? Why was I only now waking up to the dire position I had put my wife and family in? How had I missed so many signposts?

SIGNPOSTS

We're all familiar with the importance of signposts. They are meant to give us the necessary information and direction to where we're heading. They are guides and signals of where we are and what's coming up. Whether they are designed to lead us to a desired destination or warn us of upcoming difficulties, they are meant to direct and help us on our journeys.

Miss a stop sign or a red light on the road and you might cause an accident, or at minimum, get a ticket. Miss the sign for your exit off the freeway and add unnecessary time to your travels. I remember once wandering through a theme park for over an hour, trying to reconnect with my family, only to discover I had missed the key sign because I was so busy ogling my surroundings. Not even the clearest signposts can help when we're not paying attention!

Every day we are having experiences that act like signposts, trying to inform and guide us about our lives. Often, we're too hurried or preoccupied to pay them any attention. But signposts are there to serve us. So why is it that we often miss them, ignore them or race past them?

Before we jump back into my story, I'd like us to consider how easy it is for us to miss the value of the signposts in our lives. After all, without signposts, we lack direction, clues, and hints as to where we're going. Miss the wrong one and we might find ourselves in serious trouble.

WAYS WE MISS THE SIGNS

IGNORANCE- In the relationships or contexts we most often engage, it is easy to go on autopilot and fail to see the indicators desperately trying to gain our attention. This happens most easily for me in my marriage, with my children, or with my team members. Familiar contexts can make it difficult to pay attention to the details.

CONFUSION - Not all signposts are easy to understand. A few times, I have found myself driving head-on into another vehicle, only to realize I was driving the wrong direction on a one-way street! My phone map told me to take a right-hand turn, so how could I have been wrong? I have also found myself well into a harmful conversation with a friend because I wasn't able to pick up on the signs given by the other party that an unnecessary conflict was ahead.

IMPATIENCE - Have you ever been in a rush to get somewhere and you happen upon a detour sign that meant you would be late to your destination? Anger and resentment rise up and suddenly we find ourselves anxious and even taking it out on those who may be traveling with us.

ARROGANCE - I remember traveling with my family through an airport terminal when my wife suggested our gate was in the opposite direction. I laughed and assured her I had been through this airport many times and knew exactly where I was going. Even though she told me she had seen a sign indicating otherwise, I proudly led us thirty minutes in the wrong direction.

On the other hand, paying attention to, and heeding the signposts in our lives, gives us a great advantage—orientation, clarity and direction. Signposts are a gift to help us clarify where we are and where we're heading. They resolve confusion, frustration and provide the support we need to move along desirable paths. They warn us of impending trouble and reroute us toward safer paths. It is always in our best interest to pay attention and learn from the signposts in our lives.

In the story with my wife, I was clearly operating from confusion, impatience, and arrogance-the deathly trifecta! But the consequences of so many missed signposts was finally catching up to me in a way I could not ignore.

This experience will forever be etched into my memory, primarily because it was so intense and painful. We can all think back on big moments (signposts) where we've experienced something so powerful, we could not ignore it and simply move on. Our lives, in many ways, are storied and shaped by these moments. Sometimes these are positive moments like falling in love, having your first child or getting the promotion you've longed for. And sometimes these moments are negative, heartbreaking, or even tragic. The death of a loved one, the loss of a job or relationship, even discovering your star employee is leaving you can feel earth-shattering.

These big moments demand that we sit up and pay attention. They leave us no choice. Whether we like it or not, we must deal with them. This book is, in part, about how we respond to these significant moments, how we process our life experiences and make sense of them. But I want to take us deeper, to a place so few want to go.

The moment when my wife shared she wanted a separation was a really BIG moment. It couldn't be swept under the rug or causally pushed aside. The elephant in the room was no longer just in the room, it was wrecking the entire house. It wouldn't be ignored. But here's the thing: we rarely arrive at these really big moments without first having traveled through many smaller ones. These are the signposts signaling what's coming ahead. In other words, my wife didn't just wake up one day and decide she wanted a separation. There were likely hundreds, even thousands, of experiences warning us of the impending dangers. The problem is I had passed by all of these smaller experiences, scooting them under the rug until they had piled up so high we were now tripping over them. Our marriage was in jeopardy, not because of one thing that was disturbing my wife, but the many things I had become so adept at ignoring or passing over.

Let me give you some backstory.

Years prior to this moment, I was working for an organization that prided itself on a "work hard, play hard" mentality. We grew quickly, found lots of success and worked our tails off. To decompress from all the stress, many of us turned to late night parties where there was lots of drinking. In the beginning it was occasional, but over time became the norm. Some might have said our mantra had turned to "work hard, drink hard."

Many of us learned to rise early and work through hangovers. Coffee and ibuprofen became the breakfast of champions, and we thought little of it in the face of our mounting achievements. As a matter of fact, the more it became part of our team culture, the more acceptable it seemed. Our ability to drink heavily and get stuff done became an area of competence to be secretly celebrated.

During this season, my wife began sharing with me the impact of my drinking on my moods and emotional availability to our family. She also pointed out that I was snoring most nights, which kept her up and affected her ability to sleep well. I remember hearing what she was telling me, but all the while explaining these concerns away. Since others were doing the same, I couldn't be all that bad. Right?

There were so many conversations during that time about the impact of my drinking on our marriage, family, health, sex life, sleep, attitude and behaviors. They were smaller issues then, which made them easy to ignore. These were important moments lost in time, signposts I ignored in my haste to become successful. Why? Because I wasn't paying attention.

Often times, success masks deeper issues until they refuse to be hidden any longer.

Eventually, these unheeded signposts would catch up to that organization and undermine its success. What started as a shooting star ended in ashes. Often times, success masks deeper issues until they refuse to be hidden any longer.

HEEDING THE SIGNPOSTS

Sometime later, I took the helm of another organization and threw myself into my new responsibilities with fervor. With each passing month came increased stress and I eventually turned to a well-worn pathway for decompressing and managing my emotional fatigue—drinking. Again, my wife graciously tried to help me see the effects of heavy drinking on my life and leadership. I remember hearing her, but not really listening to what she was saying. I was convinced I had it under control, and because she was so close to me, she was just being overly sensitive.

There were so many more conversations with her during that season. Still, I did not recognize them for what they were—indicators that something was not right. I was driving down a busy freeway with my hair on fire and every dashboard indicator blinking red, but all I could focus on was where I was going, not how I was getting there. I was blowing past the signposts to my own peril.

Herein lies one of the major struggles any ambitious person will suffer: being unable or unwilling to recognize the importance of these smaller moments. They have so much to tell us if we could only slow down and listen. Like speed bumps, they seem more of a nuisance than anything else. We think, "Who has time to slow down when there's so much to do?" Every day, our life experiences are trying to communicate to us, warn us, teach us, even encourage us. But will we pay them attention? And here's' the kicker: life is never trying to condemn or harm us. Instead, every moment of our lives is trying to signal an opportunity, even the difficult ones.

But again, are we paying attention?

Hindsight is 20/20, so I can say this today with utter confidence: there are people who grow, transform, and increasingly contribute to the world, and there are those who don't. The difference is their willingness and ability to learn from the experiences of their lives. After all, every experience is a signpost pointing to something more significant.

Life may be painful and even seem unfair at times, but life is simply reflecting our experiences back to us, for better or worse. We are the ones who ascribe value and judgment to these experiences. Life is a neutral storyteller, giving us countless opportunities to pay attention to the signposts and make an incredibly important decision. Will we choose to pay attention and learn from our life experiences? Will we heed the signposts? Or will we condemn ourselves to repeat mistakes—plateauing our careers, destroying relationships, and suffering unnecessary consequences?

We cannot avoid all failure, but there is one we can. We can avoid the failure of learning from our life experiences. *Remember, the only true failure is failing to learn from our failures!*

The only true failure is **failing to learn from our failures!**

BACK TO THE STORY

After leading this organization for half a decade, I hit a wall. I crashed and burned. I flamed out. Truth be told, I had inherited an organization that was on the edge of death, and I was brought in to resuscitate it. Over time, the cost of change took its toll until it became clear there was no tenable future for this organization. I've learned over the years; some things are just beyond resurrection.

With the support of many mentors, I was able to lead well through the closure of this organization, but the mounting emotional cost was quickly catching up to me. The shame I felt at not being able to save this business was only compounded by my unhealthy personal habits. I found myself in a season of depression, warding off impending anxiety attacks, whilst continuing to medicate my pain. And all the while, I was missing so many signposts.

Because Kandi cares more about my health than my achievements, she continued flagging my drinking as a problem. By this point, I was staying up late most nights, drinking to escape shame and defeat. My clothes became increasingly tighter. I was easily irritable and short-tempered. Kandi and the kids walked on eggshells. Everyone around me was deeply impacted by my unhealthy coping mechanisms, but I was too self-absorbed to take note. Too often, when we're under immense pressure and struggling with coping mechanisms, we become blinded to our impact on others.

Sadly, I was convinced that *what* I was fighting for as a leader was more important than *how* I was fighting for it. I was trying to do good, but entirely unaware of all the bad that was also going on. So many more opportunities were lost in time. Why? Because I wasn't paying attention to the signposts. Understand, I truly wanted to be a good leader, a good husband, and a good father. But I would later realize that the fear of what these indicators might reveal caused me to ignore them.

Think about this. We're now talking about years and myriads of indicators trying to alert me that something wasn't right. Something wasn't working. Why did it take the threat of marital separation to make me take notice? How could I ride blind for so long? This is a question I'm sure you've asked yourself before. Why did it take so long to do something about your weight, your anger issues, your flailing career, your addiction, or your broken relationship? How is it we can overlook so many indicators until they pile up and devastate our lives?

Let me offer some suggestions that may resonate with you:

REASONS WE IGNORE THE SIGNS

BLIND SPOTS - We're just unaware. This happens. We're going through life blind to how our attitudes and behaviors are impacting ourselves and those around us. To be human is to have blind spots.

SHAME - We're embarrassed by how these indicators may reflect on us personally and therefore do whatever we can to ignore, justify, or brush them under the proverbial rug. The power of shame causes us to hide or conceal our true selves. We begin to believe our bad behavior means we're bad people. This leads to an unwillingness to deal with indicators.

DISQUALIFICATION - We're afraid the exposure of any inadequacy in us will disqualify us from desired pursuits. I desperately wanted to be a good husband to my wife, but acknowledging how my drinking was impacting her meant I had to accept that I wasn't behaving as a good husband.

LACK OF SKILLS - We're not sure what to do with these indicators. We feel ill-equipped to process these moments. We're not sure what's supposed to come out on the other side. So, we withdraw from the people who might actually help us.

FAILED ATTEMPTS - We've tried to acknowledge these moments in the past, to genuinely process them, but felt the results left us at a dead end with nowhere to go, yielding little value. We give up on our attempts to process our signposts.

REAPING AND SOWING

I'm not saying every big moment is necessarily the culmination of many smaller ones, or that all small moments will necessarily lead to a big one. What I am saying is, there is very often a correlation between the two.

Consider these real examples of leaders who failed to heed the signposts in their lives:

> One of my clients finally shares with me that her business is under water only to find out she hasn't done her books in years, has no understanding of cash flow and suddenly realizes she's in a heap of debt. She continues to borrow more money until the bank cuts her off and she loses her business.
>
> Another client consistently vents his frustration at particular team members, saying they are too young, entitled and needy. Then one day, they all walk out, leaving him with too many balls to juggle. His business suffers greatly.

A board member ignores the many complaints about how he speaks to other board members. They share how they often feel belittled and scorned by him. He wakes up to an email letting him know he's been fired from the board.

A friend complains about her misguided teenagers, saying they are entitled and spoiled, and how every attempt to control their behavior fails. She considers family counseling but convinces herself she's too busy. She would find out years later that it was her workaholism that drove her husband and kids from her life.

Another client ignores the indicators of significant weight-gain, sleepless nights, high levels of stress and constant pain in his shoulder. He says he has no time to see a doctor. He has a massive heart attack requiring a four-way bypass that alters his life forever.

A husband ignores the many indicators that his excessive drinking is deeply impacting his marriage and family, but he's too busy changing the world to take notice, until his wife requests a separation (Yes, I'm referring to myself).

Each of these stories is an example of a failure to pay attention to the smaller issues until they compounded into much bigger ones!

We've all heard the saying, "You reap what you sow." We understand our decisions and behaviors have natural consequences, sometimes for better and sometimes for worse. The problem begins when we're not paying attention to what we're sowing or reaping. In my situation, years went by when I was unaware of (or willfully ignoring) the indicators I was sowing toward a separation. Of course,

> **We can learn to see every experience as a goldmine, ready to be plundered for our benefit, to become and contribute to a better version of ourselves.**

in any given moment, I would have explained to you how the drinking was a justifiable coping mechanism enabling me to push through stress and fight for important things.

I hope you hear the irony in that statement!

As humans, whatever our responsibilities in life may be, we are responsible for what we sow and reap. Unfortunately, it can take us far too long to realize the harvest we're actually sowing. Often, it's not until the consequences are dire that we wake up and realize we've been sowing toward irreparable outcomes.

For this reason, we find ourselves:

- stuck in patterns of unhelpful behaviors
- plateauing in our growth
- frustrated with where we are in life
- convincing ourselves that the world will never play fair
- believing we're doomed to failure and disappointment

Thankfully, this book is about transforming even the most difficult moments of our lives so they work for us, not against us. And we don't have to wait for cataclysmic consequences to pay attention. We can learn to see every experience as a goldmine, ready to be plundered for our benefit, to become and contribute to a better version of ourselves.

But first, we must learn to seize these moments before they seize us.

02

SEIZING OUR MOMENTS

I have often been asked, "Eric, how do you muster the courage to tackle your greatest failures when there is so much at stake?" Or, let's apply that question to my opening story. How did I muster the courage to take responsibility for my own inadequacies, when it would have been easier to go on blaming my wife for why the marriage wasn't working?"

The answer to that question is simple to understand, but incredibly difficult to practice.

Years ago, a mentor spoke some very challenging words to me in the midst of my complaining about a relationship. He said, "Eric, relationships are not 50/50, but 100/100. Each party is responsible to take 100% responsibility for their attitudes and behaviors. Doing this requires that we give up our incessant need to be right or blame others, and instead focus on what we can learn from these experiences. Posturing yourself as a learner means you have endless growth available to you. On the other hand, following your need to be right means you already know everything and have ceased learning."

I knew back then I wanted to be a learner, someone who has endless opportunity for growth and transformation. What I didn't know was how often it would require surrendering my need to blame others for my attitudes and behaviors, and how painfully humbling it is to look squarely at the most broken parts of who I am.

Let's be honest, no one likes to see where they suck!

My courage to practice personal responsibility, in what feels like humiliating circumstances, comes from my experience of what comes out on the other side. I am qualitatively a very different human today from even one year ago. I am a far better version of myself because I made a decision to do everything in my power to pay attention to signposts (even when it takes me a while to wake up to them). I am more of an asset to any environment today because of the many times I have chosen personal responsibility over the self-protecting defense of fighting to be right. I am who I am today and will continue to grow because I choose every day to be a learner.

A good friend once said to me, "The path that at first looks like it leads to life, often leads to death. And the path that at first looks like it leads to death, actually leads to life." The path of self-protection looks like a lifeline at first, but is the rope of fear and pride we inevitably hang ourselves with. The path of personal responsibility often feels terrifying at first, like a death-sentence, but always gives us opportunity to learn and grow.

My courage to step into my own failures in our marriage is actually what put me back into the driver's seat of my own life.

Yes, this is counterintuitive, but from years of experience, I can tell you it's the path we've all been looking for. It's the path that leads to the life we most long for— a path of freedom to continually become who we were meant to be.

CARPE DIEM

We've all heard the phrase, *carpe diem*, translated "seize the day." The Roman poet Horace was encouraging us to consider the brevity of life—that we cannot control the world around us, and therefore we should enjoy every moment for what it is. In a similar way, I am imploring you to join me in the adventure of learning to seize every moment of your life for what it is: an opportunity to transform every experience into learning, growth and becoming a better version of yourself. Instead of ignoring the signposts, hoping life will mysteriously turn out, we can recognize and learn from them.

Today is the day!

That's right, we can develop the skills to lay hold of every experience in our lives and to make sure they are serving us. This journey will require that we audit our mindset, take personal responsibility for our trajectory and believe that life is happening *for* us, not *to* us. We must learn to seize our moments or they will certainly seize us.

We must learn to seize our moments or they will certainly seize us.

As children, we were wide-eyed and full of imagination. The world seemed endless with possibilities. We could do anything and become anything. The world was our oyster! We believed the world was for us; an open horizon full of amazing adventures. Then pain enters our story. This is the human predicament. We experience broken promises, dysfunctional relationships, forms of abuse, disappointment, failure and heartache... Our view of the world is tarnished. Consequently, our perspective changes too. The impact of difficult life moments (or seasons) often has the effect of making us more cynical, cautious and even fearful of the next painful moment.

After working with leaders for almost two decades, most of them can think back to various experiences that jaded their view of the world, and even themselves. Little by little, we become suspicious of our life experiences. We believe they have the power to determine who we are and what will become of us. A victim mentality slowly seeps in, and we live more and more reactively, desperate to navigate the minefield of unpredictable disappointments.

It's natural that we develop coping mechanisms to self-protect from potentially difficult experiences. As children, we refuse to join a game because someone has mocked our lack of athleticism. Or we avoid speaking up in class because someone previously ridiculed us. As adults, we may have grown older, but we still seek to protect our fragile inner-person. We avoid a particular coworker on account of their difficult personality. We avoid our boss for fear they will expose a failure. We sidestep conflict for fear it will blow up in our faces. We neglect having hard conversations to escape painful outcomes. Sadly, it's our avoidance of difficult situations that often compound those situations into greater difficulty.

During childhood, we developed coping mechanisms that served us by shielding our hearts and minds where others did not (or could not). However, in our adulthood, these same coping mechanisms can undermine us, causing us to over- or under-function. What may have saved us as children now sabotages us as adults. Coping mechanisms can be subtle, like conflict avoidance, gossip, isolation, passivity, or harboring an inner grudge. They can also be more aggressive, like fits of anger, sarcasm, biting comments, power struggles or physical intimidation. Whatever coping mechanisms we lean toward, they do not help us resolve issues; they only exacerbate them.

As we progress through our lives, we need new mechanisms that empower us to tackle whatever life may throw at us. We need practical ways of navigating the best and worst experiences so we can become *more* of who we are meant to be, not less.

We've all seen how hurdlers run shorter distances while leaping continuously over each obstacle. Could you imagine running a marathon this way? But that's how life often feels, like we're continuously hurdling over life experiences for fear of how they will impact us. Life doesn't have to be this way. I'm not saying we don't have to deal with certain moments of our lives and avoid every hurdle. But I am saying we can meet with every obstacle in a way that serves us, rather than threatens us.

Everything changes the moment you realize YOU actually have the authority to make every experience in life work for you.

That's right, you're not a victim. As a human being, within you is a much greater power. *Whether these experiences are big, small, positive or negative, you and I get to choose what we make of them.* This is our superpower!

TAPPING INTO OUR POWER

Of course, we can't control the world around us, nor can we mitigate against all pain and suffering. But real freedom and power comes when we develop the ability to seize every impactful experience of our lives as an amazing opportunity, rather than a threat. You and I are the captains of our own journey—the heroes of our own story—when we choose to take 100% personal responsibility for our own lives.

Years ago, I discovered the key that put me back in the driver's seat of my own life: *Who we are today and how we operate is actually a byproduct of how we process and make sense of our life experiences, not the events themselves.* When we think life is happening to us, our job is to cope with it, even survive it. We become fatalistic, believing our experiences will determine who we are and what becomes of us. A bad boss means we'll never get promoted. A divorce means we're doomed to life alone. A failed startup means we're not entrepreneurs. But remember, life is not what happens to us as much as what we make of it.

> *Listen carefully—we, not our life experiences,*
> *are in the driver's seat of our future.*

For this reason, two people can go through the same event, but come out on the other end with very different interpretations of their experience. How each makes sense of their experience will determine how they see themselves and the world around them. For example, two people are let go in a company-wide layoff. One determines the company has acted unfairly and believes authority figures cannot be trusted. They drag their feet in looking for other work, telling themselves the next boss will be the same. The other person, though saddened at the news, is grateful for the experience and believes it will prepare them for their next opportunity. They jump into their job search with anticipation and hope, believing they will find something better. While the first person is playing the victim, the second person is in the driver's seat, functioning with authority and power over their own life. The first person sees life happening *to* them, the second sees life happening *for* them.

Our life experiences—past or present—do not get to define us or determine our future. Only we have that authority. The secret unveiled in this book is that we have the choice to interpret and assign meaning to our experiences. We get to determine what we make of our experiences, rather than letting them make something of us. We get to choose how we process every moment of our lives, which puts learning, growth, and purpose into our hands. This is the mindset shift required if we're going to move out of the victim mindset and take our lives back, one moment at a time.

> **Tapping into your authority and power begins with rejecting a victim mentality.**

Tapping into your authority and power begins with rejecting a victim mentality and taking personal responsibility for our attitudes and behaviors. This postures us to excavate the most valuable commodity found in every life experience—wisdom.

IN PURSUIT OF WISDOM

Most of us spent years in some type of formal education. We may have received high school diplomas, and even pursued graduate studies. I call this academic learning. We consume information with the expectation that we can recall it during an exam. The focus during these formal years of education is largely information acquisition and regurgitation. There is no doubt about the value of this type of learning. We need lots of information to operate in our world.

But there is another type of learning, one that is not often taught in the classroom—*wisdom learning*. Wisdom learning is different to academic learning in that it cannot be acquired primarily from books, seminars and the like. Wisdom learning is squeezed from our life experiences when we begin to make the connection between *what* happened and *why* it happened. If academic learning is focused on the *what* of how the world works, wisdom learning is focused on *why* the world works the way it does. Academic learning gives us context for the problems we experience. From there, we may see things more accurately, but wisdom learning gives us access to the underlying reasons behind that experience.

For example, we may have a blow up with our significant other and apologize for our outbursts the next day without understanding why things got so heated in the first place. We may feel ourselves constantly irked by a coworker in meetings, so we avoid them, but not understand what specifically is frustrating us about them. Very often, leaders come to us with *what* is bothering them, but with little understanding of *why*.

Wisdom learning helps us interpret *why* things are the way they are; why we respond upset, irritated, afraid, insecure, stressed and anxious. Wisdom learning gives us opportunity, not only to identify our problems, but to source where those problems are stemming from. Until we can see the *why*, we'll find ourselves stuck in the *what*.

Until we can see the *why,* we'll find ourselves stuck in the *what.*

EXPERIENCE IS OUR ALLY

Consider the difference between the new and the experienced mechanic. The new mechanic has learned all about cars, has received certifications, has studied diagrams, but has minimum experience working on cars themselves. The more experienced mechanic draws not only on their learned information but also on their wisdom gained from having worked on lots of cars. They have developed the ability to diagnose signposts and the systemic problems that are invisible to the newer mechanic. This is why more experienced people can solve problems far more readily than their novice counterparts. For this reason, a trusted mechanic is worth their weight in gold! The wise mechanic not only sees the facts, they are also able to interpret them through the lens of previous experiences and identify the systemic issues that are causing the problems. This is their superpower.

I often remind the new coaches we train that no matter how well they know our tools, there is no substitute for reps. The more they coach, the better they become. Why? Experience solving problems leads to increased wisdom. They are more effective in their ability to diagnose a client's situation and help them see the relevant factors hiding beneath the surface. It's not until we understand the cause of our problems that we can begin to solve them.

> **It's not until we understand the cause of our problems that we can begin to solve them.**

Today, technology is leveling the playing field. When we take our car to the mechanic, they plug our car into a diagnostic device that immediately gives them a read out on what's working and what's not working. The diagnostic tool helps them understand the inner workings of the car, which in turn makes their ability to fix problems more accurate and expedient.

What if we had a diagnostic tool that could help us see beneath the hood of our own lives, revealing the systemic issues that are both helping or hindering us? Isn't this why we go to therapists? I'm a huge advocate for the value of good therapists, but we still need a tool that equips us to make sense of our lives on a daily basis so that we can better make sense of, and solve, our own problems.

One of our coaches is an experienced trauma therapist who oversees a large counseling practice. I first met him when he joined our coaching process. When he learned the tool revealed in this book, he said to me, "Eric, we help people process the most impactful experiences of their lives, but until this tool, we didn't have a way of equipping them to do this for themselves. Now we do." Today, all of his counselors are not only equipped with this tool, but relish the opportunity to empower clients with it as well.

When my wife confronted me about a possible separation, it wasn't good enough to say sorry. There was no quick fix. My only option was to take a hard look beneath the hood of my own life and see what I could learn. I had read tons of books on relationships and marriage, but I needed more than just good information. I needed to grow in wisdom. I needed to understand what was beneath the painful symptoms in my marriage, diagnose the cause of my attitudes and behaviors, and make systemic changes that would lead to sustainable outcomes. Without access to wisdom, I would only ever put a Band-Aid on a broken engine.

For too many of us, we find ourselves trapped on a merry-go-round of unresolved problems and negative patterns of behavior. We're going round and round, hoping somehow we'll magically find ourselves in a better place. Over time, we begin to believe our problems are mysteries that cannot be solved. This is where we fall prey to the temptations of quitting what we're doing, looking for "greener grass," or settling for what we have. I get it! Life is hard, but it doesn't have to be an endless journey through a never-ending desert of repeat disappointments and frustrations.

That's not the life we're settling for. We want something better. Right?

In our experience, leaders are not lacking in intelligence or education. What they are lacking is a simple mechanism for identifying, addressing and solving real time problems. Without such a mechanism, we will avoid, circumvent, abdicate or "command and control" our way through challenges. But we know this doesn't work, at least not for long. Small problems become large ones. Conflict and tensions go unresolved and wreak havoc in our relationships. Trust is broken. Communication is stifled. Progress is slowed or completely halted.

Sound familiar?

> Take a minute and think about this season of your life. Are there signposts you've been ignoring? Are you navigating the consequences of missed signposts? Where are you feeling stuck, overwhelmed or underwater? What if you could flip the script on these experiences and make them work for you?

BENEATH THE SURFACE

Wisdom is our ability to understand why things are the way they are and how to respond effectively. Our clients don't hire us to point out their problems; they already know! They bring us in to help them diagnose the source of their problems and discover simple, effective solutions. And the best solutions always begin in the same place—at the root of our problems.

Let's dig a bit deeper.

In the diagram below, we see that information is associated with what we see happening above the surface, in the visible realm, where we can make observations and gather data and details. Wisdom asks the necessary questions to help us understand what's happening beneath the surface, in the invisible realm. Seeing beneath the surface gives us access to the systemic elements producing the symptoms above the surface. Wisdom is our ability to identify the *why* causing the *what*. In the words of a good friend, "if you want good fruits, you gotta have good roots!"

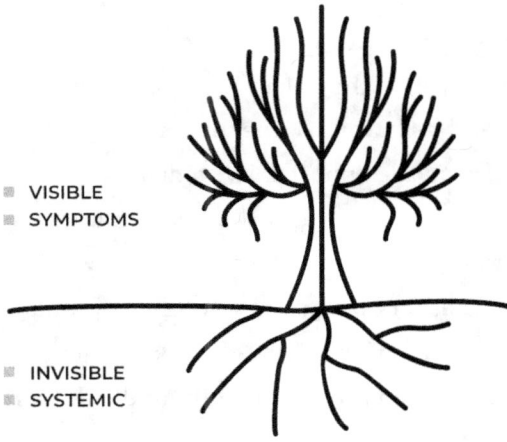

- VISIBLE
- SYMPTOMS

- INVISIBLE
- SYSTEMIC

In my work with leaders and organizations, I draw this diagram to help them understand why we suffer from repeat problems and plateau in our growth. We can spend all the time we want addressing the symptoms, failing to affect change because we're not addressing the systemic issues driving those very symptoms.

This is why, with access to more information than we've ever had, leaders lament how spreadsheets, reports and analyses don't necessarily translate into better decisions and outcomes. This book is about understanding the relationship between the systemic and the symptomatic dimensions of our lives and leadership. We'll learn how to diagnose the problems we experience with the purpose of making the necessary systemic changes that will result in more desirable outcomes. *In other words, we'll learn to make the internal changes that will greatly impact our external experiences.*

GOOD ROOTS = GOOD FRUITS.

In my story with my wife, countless symptoms had been brought to my attention. But they were wasted on my unwillingness to slow down and ask what deeper issues they were revealing to me. I was missing the opportunity to discover what was going on beneath the surface. Instead, I was busy blaming everyone and everything around me for what wasn't working. I was failing to see how *my* attitudes and behaviors were the byproduct of what was happening internally. I was failing to take personal responsibility, and therefore, missed the opportunity to dig deeper in pursuit of wisdom.

And this is the same for teams and organizations. We experience challenges, setbacks, failures and frustrations, but our greatest failure is not learning from these moments. We're not sure how to make the connection between the visible and invisible, the symptomatic and the systemic, the signposts and the deeper issues. So, we do our best to address what we can see, look for quick fixes, and miss out on the deep, sustainable change that is available.

I've never met anyone who looks forward to an MRI scan. Spending countless minutes sardined inside a claustrophobia-inducing machine is nobody's idea of a good time! But when the doctor says we need an MRI scan, we do it. Why? Because we trust that the discomfort we feel in the process will reveal the much-needed data to help the doctor diagnose our symptoms. The tool we'll learn in this book is like an MRI machine. It will help us see what's going on inside our lives and leadership. It will reveal what is helpful and unhelpful about how we view ourselves and the world around us. Understand this, the tool makes no judgement; its purpose is to help us see what we could not before see. Then, and only then, can we make the necessary changes that lead to greater outcomes for everyone involved. After all, *we can only change what we can first see.*

After all, we *can only change what we can first see.*

Taking back the driver's seat of our everyday lives is something we can all learn. Instead of ignoring, circumventing, or constantly feeling overwhelmed by our life experiences, we'll learn to:

1. Identify them for what they are—simply opportunities for personal and even corporate learning, growth and transformation.

2. Own the emotions that arise in any experience as helpful indicators of what's going on inside us.

3. Process our experiences in a way that serves, rather than undermines us.

4. Transform any moment, even the toughest, into a goldmine of life and leadership intelligence.

5. Engage anything life throws at us and turn it into a pathway marked by clarity, confidence and courage.

The journey ahead is guaranteed to push our limits and test our inner mettle. We'll learn to practice radical honesty, embrace humility and believe in a better version of ourselves. Instead of sidestepping moments of our lives, we'll learn to seize them and transform them to serve us.

Remember, this is your superpower. You have it within you.

We've trained thousands of leaders in these skills and have seen lives and companies transformed from the inside out. Thankfully, unlocking your superpower does not require being bit by a radioactive insect. Instead, it begins with learning to see every experience in life as just another KAIROS!

A *what*?

03
KAIROS MOMENTS

That's a funny word. What is a Kairos? This word comes from the Ancient Greek language and is one of two words used for "time." Chronos is the word we're more familiar with, from which we get the word chronological. This is sequential time, stopwatch time, calendar time, or linear time. This kind of time passes second by second and provides us with a timeline on which we can plot our entrance and exit from the world stage and everything in between.

The other word the Greeks have for time is Kairos. Kairos time is defined as significant moments where conditions are right for critical action. These are opportune or decisive moments begging to be recognized and responded to.[1] Kairos moments are pregnant with experiences and opportunity. Other scholars define Kairos as the "right time;" a significant moment that sets itself apart amidst our Chronos timeline.

---

1 https://www.merriam-webster.com/dictionary/kairos

I like to think of Kairos moments as hinge moments, where we have the opportunity to make decisions that will affect our trajectory.

See the diagram below.

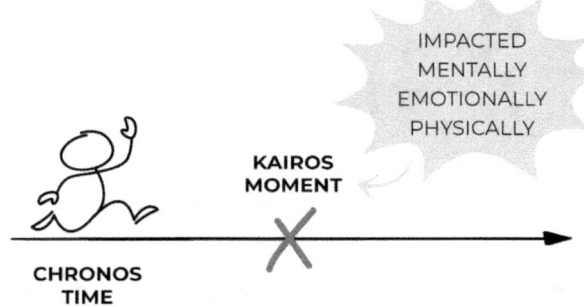

A Kairos moment (frequently referred to as a trigger) is any experience along our chronological journey, big or small, positive or negative, when we are impacted mentally, emotionally or physically. I'll bet you've identified plenty of Kairos moments in your life without knowing there is a word for it! Maybe you've said something like, "Remember that amazing dinner we enjoyed at the rooftop restaurant?" Or, "Remember when our kids were little and wouldn't stay in their beds at night?" Or, "Remember when I lost my temper with the TSA worker for emptying my suitcase in search of a weapon that ended up being my metal nail file (true story)?"

A Kairos moment is any experience in life that stands out, grabs our attention and impacts us, for better or worse. It could be a comment from a coworker or a look your boss gives you. It could be seeing a flood of red lights ahead of you on the freeway or that innocent smile and hug your toddler gives you as you leave for work. Big or small, positive or negative, Kairos moments are happening every day and impacting our internal state of being.

The smaller or positive Kairos moments are easily overlooked. Meanwhile, the larger, negative ones can trigger and derail us. Either way, if we don't confidently know what to do with Kairos moments, we tend to pass them by, scoot them under the rug or shove them into a closet. Unfortunately, when you push enough stuff under the rug, you eventually start tripping over it. Like we've already seen, unattended smaller Kairos moments can pile up until they eventually blow up in our faces!

In the words of David Allen, "If you don't pay appropriate attention to what has your attention, it will take more of your attention than it deserves."

I think the Greeks were on to something, understanding the importance in their language of differentiating between Chronos and Kairos time. We get so easily caught up in Chronos time and forget to pay attention to Kairos moments. Where Chronos is quantitative, Kairos is qualitative and experiential. We've become so hurried, moving from event to event and hustling about in pursuit of achievement. We can easily lose sight of the moments in time that are actually shaping who we are, who we're becoming, and how we're impacting the world around us.

We've heard it said we can miss the forest for the trees. True. But, in this case we're missing the trees for the forest. We're blazing through life at breakneck speed and missing hundreds, even thousands, of incredible moments that are begging to be recognized, explored and excavated for what they offer—invaluable life wisdom. Simply put, Kairos moments are the signposts alerting us to life's learning opportunities.

Don't worry, we won't forget about the forest in this process. Instead, we'll learn how to make sense of the forest by paying a bit more attention to the unique landscape found therein. Each moment in our lives represents a part of the larger whole. The better we can make sense of the Kairos moments the better we understand our Chronos journey!

Consider my opening story. I was missing the incredible turbulence I was creating in our marriage because I wasn't paying attention to the smaller Kairos moments that were inevitably leading to a very big one!

CHANGE YOUR TRAJECTORY

Over the twenty years of coaching leaders at every level and from a vast array of industries, I have discovered one very important thing that separates the leaders who continue to grow from those who don't. It is this: their ability to identify and process Kairos moments effectively, especially the more impactful ones. What we'll discover together is—whether positive or negative—every Kairos is an opportunity to learn from life and transform our trajectory.

> **Every Kairos is an opportunity to learn from life and transform our trajectory.**

We've only gotten this far in life because we've developed some capability to cope with or move past Kairos moments. As you can see in the diagram below, when a big enough Kairos hits or enough smaller ones pile up, we can easily become hijacked and find ourselves mentally and emotionally derailed. And suddenly we find our trajectory has changed for the worse. When we're hijacked, we find ourselves operating from fear, anger, resentment, insecurity or shame. We become a shadow of our best selves and a liability to our environment.

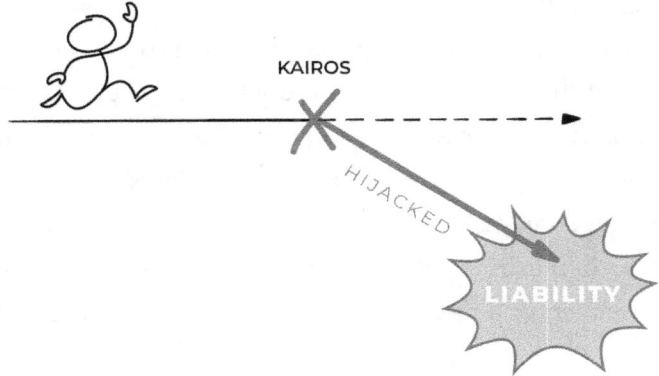

A common response when hijacked is to take on a victim or villain mindset. We either withdraw from life and throw ourselves a pity party, or we try to make the world around us conform to our will. Both reflect self-protecting mechanisms and only compound our problems.

If we're not paying attention, we'll find more and more of our lives reflecting this lower trajectory until some parts feel unrecoverable. Sometimes we're too busy to pay attention. Other times, we're convinced there is no better way.

> Take a moment and see if you can identify any areas of your own life that reflect the liability trajectory. How did you get there? How do you feel about these areas of your life? Don't just read on. Take a minute and think about this.

The good news is there is an alternative pathway available to us in every Kairos moment. We call it the Pathway of Personal Responsibility. Remember, our life experiences do not get to determine who we are and how we operate. We are the only ones who get to make that choice! We get to seize every Kairos and take 100% personal responsibility for what we learn and how we respond to any Kairos moment. By doing this, we reject the victim or villain mindset that so easily strangles us. This is how we put the best version of ourselves back in the driver's seat. By doing this, we become an asset to our environment and choose a better future for ourselves and others.

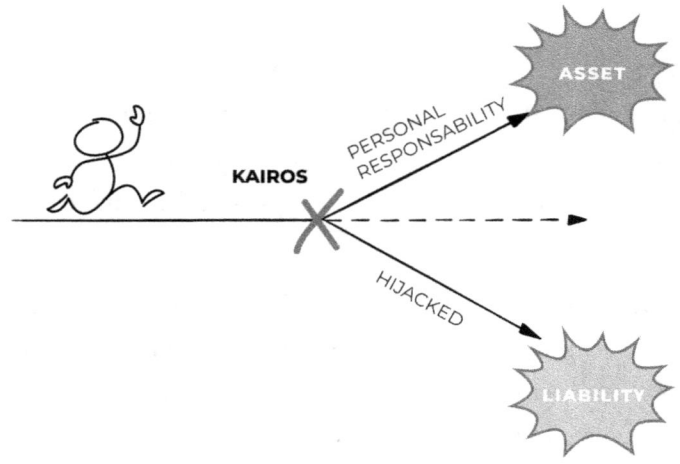

We cannot choose at which point we enter the grand chronological timeline of history, nor can we choose every experience in between, but we do get to choose how we engage and respond to every moment of our lives. And here's more good news: our lives are shaped more by what we *can* choose than by what we *can't*. I may not get to choose what country I was born in, or the family I was born into, but I get to choose what I make of all life circumstances. I don't always get to choose my boss, co-workers, clients and the people I interact with every day, but I get to choose how I engage with them.

Here's more good news: our lives are shaped more by what we *can* choose than by what we *can't*.

Remember, too many of us approach life as if it were happening *to us*. We become victims of our experiences, blaming the world for what's not going our way. Our only option in this mindset is to complain, waiting for the world to conform to our expectations. This robs us of our agency and our opportunity to contribute a better version of ourselves to any environment.

Years ago, I learned the freedom and power of living from what I call a Kairos Mindset, where we welcome the growth afforded us in each Kairos moment. A Kairos Mindset sets us free to recognize that life is actually happening *for* us, not *to* us. Life is what we make of it, not what it makes of us. The victim mindset disempowers us, but the Kairos Mindset empowers us to lay hold of every experience as an opportunity to choose our trajectory. Who would have thought that a little ol' word like "Kairos" could make such a big difference!

The invitation in what I'm saying can be illustrated below as we move from a mindset that life is happening *to* us to one where it is happening *for* us. When we make this transition, we'll find that the best things in life begin to happen *through* us!

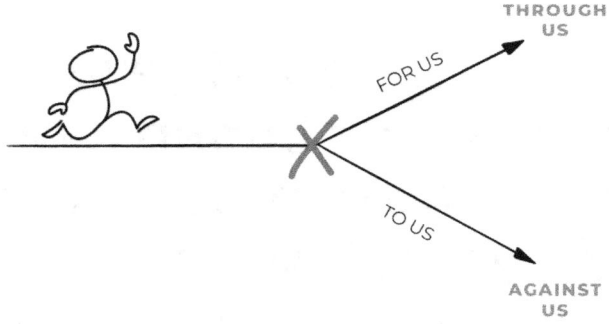

Every Kairos, no matter how challenging, is an opportunity to choose our trajectory!

Every Kairos, no matter how challenging, is an opportunity to choose our trajectory!

And that means every life experience really is an incredible opportunity! Even the most difficult situations become a treasure hunt for learning and growth: an opportunity to slow down, see our experiences for what they are and make decisions born out of mental and emotional clarity. Who doesn't want that?!

A TRANSFORMATIONAL TOOL

The tool we'll learn together is called the Kairos Circle. It is adapted from the work of a former mentor who taught me the importance of developing tools that help us practice the best version of ourselves, even under great pressure[2]. We lovingly refer to the Kairos Circle as the Swiss Army Knife of our toolkit because it is incredibly versatile in its application. Most importantly, the Kairos Circle empowers us to transform every life and leadership obstacle into a better outcome for everyone involved.

My team of coaches have often heard me say that if there was only one tool I could use in my coaching, this would be it! Why? Because the use of this tool literally transforms the way we see and engage ourselves and the world. It transforms individuals and groups. It transforms paradigms and culture. It transforms the way we think and the way we behave. It greatly enhances our self-awareness and our ability to interact with others more effectively. It increases clarity, fuels confidence and releases fresh courage in the face of any challenge. Quite simply, this tool changes everything, especially your trajectory.

Our coaching business is fully committed to developing tools and practices that move the needle of human performance. We understand the engine of any business is its people, how they operate individually and corporately. This tool is part of a core toolkit we have developed to help leaders and organizations take

---

2   *Building a Discipling Culture,* Breen, 2011.

human performance to radical new levels. The Kairos Circle is not just a great idea, it is a necessary acquisition if we're going to take our own performance to new heights!

In this book we'll begin with the core application of the tool, which is to identify and process your own Kairos moments. We call this Self-Coaching, which is the gateway to transformed leadership. We'll then spend some time covering other key applications such as:

1. COACHING OTHERS - Use this tool to help others identify and process their Kairos moments to change their trajectory. This application will help you become the best coaching leader.

2. COLLABORATIVE PROBLEM-SOLVING - Learn how every problem or decision facing a person or team is just another Kairos to be processed, learned from and responded to. This application unlocks the collective genius in any team.

3. CONFLICT ENGAGEMENT - Learn how every conflict is just another Kairos moment, begging to be processed with the intent of learning together with others and discovering win-win solutions. This application flips the script on conflict from threat to opportunity.

4. REVIEWING PEOPLE AND PROJECTS - Learn the most effective way to review any person, event, or project, with the purpose of promoting growth and development. This application unlocks the human potential within any individual or group.

MATRIX MOMENTS

As you learn the Kairos Circle, you'll begin to have what I call "Matrix Moments." You may remember in the original Matrix[3] movie, the main character, Neo (played by Keanu Reeves), has grown suspicious of the reality he's living in, that it's actually a facade, a projection of a deeper reality hidden from common view. In a similar way, the Kairos Circle will open your eyes to see the hidden factors shaping your life experiences, and more importantly how you interpret your experiences and respond to them. Every Kairos will become a portal through which you will see the matrix of your life and get to choose your desired trajectory.

As in the movie, seeing the matrix isn't the end goal; learning how to respond effectively to the matrix is. The Kairos Circle will offer you a step-by-step process to see beneath the surface of any experience and understand why it's happening. You will learn to excavate meaning, significance and wisdom from each journey around the Kairos Circle. You'll discover the power of how our internal belief systems are driving our attitudes and behaviors. You'll even learn to exchange old, unhelpful beliefs for new, empowering ones. You will also learn how to cultivate what you learn through simple plans that lead to sustainable transformation.

At first, the tool might feel clumsy, because it's new to you. Let me encourage you with this—in your best moments, you actually practice the Kairos Circle. Here's how: this tool is only a reflection of how humans process their lives when they are operating at their

---

3 The Matrix– Warner Brothers, Roadshow Entertainment; 1999

best. The Kairos Circle won't teach you something foreign to yourself. The magic is in the fact that it will clarify and reinforce how to best engage life experiences, especially when under pressure. The more comfortable you become with this tool, the easier it will be for you to identify Kairos moments and move forward with newfound courage.

Every tool I share with leaders must solve many problems to prove worthy of our time and energy. As the world grows increasingly complex, tools help us navigate the ever-changing landscape. We need a simple tool that clarifies the understanding of our challenges and leads us to effective solutions. The Kairos Circle does just that. With its simple framework, we will find ourselves confidently equipped to solve our problems, learning from every success and failure.

Our goal is to turn every life experience, positive or negative, into our increased wisdom.

Now, into the matrix we go!

PART TWO

THE KAIROS CIRCLE

TWO CRUCIAL QUESTIONS

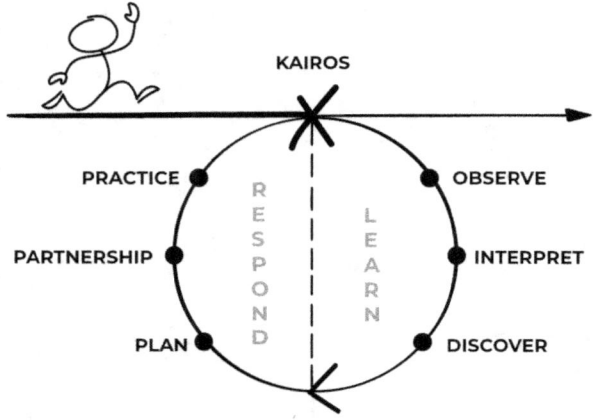

The Kairos Circle offers a simple, visual framework that empowers us to practice identifying and processing Kairos moments. Before we dive in, let's quickly consider the two main questions this tool will help us navigate for any Kairos moment:

1. **WHAT AM I LEARNING?** Every Kairos moment is an opportunity to learn about ourselves, others and our circumstances. The Kairos Circle will help us connect the dots between the symptoms we experience and the systemic issues going on beneath the surface. We'll not only learn to pay greater attention to *what* is happening but also to *why* it's happening, so we can take 100% personal responsibility for our attitudes and behaviors. We'll explore the mindsets and beliefs that often unwittingly shape how we see and respond to our experiences. In my book,

Leadership Gravitas[4], we talked about this through the practice of self-awareness. The Kairos Circle will help us increase our self-awareness so that we're no longer flying blind or living reactively.

2. HOW WILL I RESPOND? Every Kairos moment will offer us an opportunity to choose our trajectory with clear and decisive plans that consider what's in the best interest for all parties involved. In Leadership Gravitas we referred to this as the practice of self-leadership. The Kairos Circle will help us develop our self-leadership so that we're owning our personal trajectory and how we're impacting others.

---

[4] Leadership Gravitas, copyright 2021

04

IDENTIFYING OUR KAIROS MOMENTS

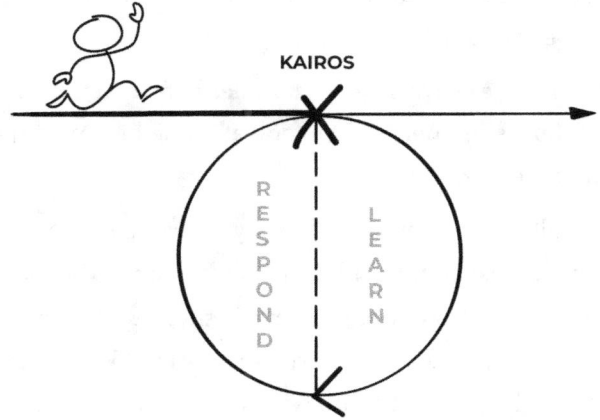

Our first order of business is learning how to identify Kairos moments and determine which ones deserve our time and attention. After all, we can't possibly process every Kairos we have as there are too many. However, we can learn to identify those which promise to yield the most learning and growth.

Let's remember a Kairos is any moment in your life that impacts you mentally, emotionally or physically. They can be large or small, positive or negative. Kairos moments are most easily spotted by the emotions they trigger. Anytime we're experiencing heightened emotions we're likely having a Kairos moment.

We've been identifying Kairos moments our entire lives; we just didn't call them by this name. Anytime a friend asks you how things are going, they are inquiring about the Kairos moments of your life. At night, before bed, we often ask our significant others how their day was; this is soliciting Kairos moments. Even the dentist will look for Kairos moments when they ask if you've experienced any pain in your mouth recently or how that last crown is feeling. Kairos moments are the signposts signaling there is something deeper at hand.

Just so we've got plenty of examples before we ask you to identify your Kairos moments, let's look at some big and small Kairos moments together.

- I still remember over twenty years ago when my older brother asked me if I loved my girlfriend. My heart jumped into my throat. I stammered, stuttered and finally broke out with, "I do love her!" That was a Kairos moment. I didn't know what to do with it at the moment, but I knew something big was brewing. Those words erupting from my mouth meant my life would never be the same. Kandi and I married shortly thereafter.

- I remember when my wife showed me our first positive pregnancy test. I would be a father! I was overwhelmed. This was a Kairos. No clue what to do with this Kairos, but my trajectory was shifting.

- The day I finished grad school and received my diploma was another powerful Kairos. I felt utter relief after spending years balancing a young family, a full-time job and a full class load.

- Signing our first sizable contract for MPWR Coaching and holding our first published book in hand were also powerful Kairos moments.

Many of us would consider these big Kairos moments, even life-altering ones.

Raising children, getting a dream job, moving to a new city, getting fired, breaking up with your significant other, riding through endless turbulence wondering whether the plane will crash—these are all considered big Kairos moments. But what about the littler ones? As I said earlier, our tendency is to over-focus on the larger Kairos moments at the expense of the smaller ones. Regardless of their size, every Kairos moment is a signpost alerting us to an important opportunity to decide our trajectory.

Let me share some examples of smaller Kairos moments that may also prove worthy of our attention.

- I remember leaving the house one morning and hearing from the bedroom, "Babe, don't forget you're taking your son to volleyball practice at 6pm." I responded with a quick, "Yep, no problem." As I drove away from the house I thought, *Oh crap, I've booked an afternoon round of golf. I can't possibly do both!* That's a Kairos. Maybe not life altering (Kandi may disagree), but still a considerable oversight that would require some action.

- How about the time we hosted a work party at our house, and I barked at my daughter in front of some guests because she wasn't dropping everything to help me in my distress? Yep, that was a Kairos. For me it was a small Kairos, but I would later learn it was a biggie for my daughter. This would certainly require some attention.

- Recently, my wife generously dropped me off at the airport for a very early flight. When we arrived, my stress levels skyrocketed as the line of cars for departures was so long, I couldn't even see the terminal! Was it my insistence on grabbing a Starbucks on the way that put me in this predicament? Either way, I was having a Kairos moment. I made my flight, but determined it was a Kairos worthy of processing because I didn't appreciate starting my journey in a stressful state.

Other small and notable Kairos moments may look like: banging your toes on a piece of furniture you've sworn for months to move; spilling coffee on yourself in the car because you've failed to buy a travel mug (or find the lost lid); incurring a late fine for a bill you could have set up on automatic payment; showing up late to yet another meeting because you do not give yourself enough lead time. They may seem small in the grand scheme of things, but these are the types of Kairos moments that offer us a chance to learn something valuable. Matter of fact, while working with high-level leaders, these smaller Kairos moments often find their way into our conversations and can reveal important insights about how they've been operating.

CHARTING YOUR KAIROS MOMENTS

Ok, now it's your turn. I've shared a variety of examples of Kairos moments from my life. Here's your first assignment. In the space below I'd like you to think back on the last month or so, and identify Kairos moments in the left column. In the second column, describe them as big or small. In the third column identify them as positive or negative. There's no judgment or wrong answers here, so write down whatever comes to your mind. Don't worry about the final column; we'll tackle that next.

(Note - Feel free to write in the space provided below or record them elsewhere. We'll be doing a variety of these types of exercises together, so I suggest you do the work and record it somewhere!)

KAIROS	BIG OR SMALL	POSITIVE OR NEGATIVE	SCORE (1–5)

The next part of this assignment is to give each Kairos a score based on how important you think that Kairos is to process and learn from. This may be determined by the accompanying emotions, its apparent significance, or its impact on your life. This is our way of prioritizing Kairos moments when we have many.

1 = Not So Important

5 = Very Important

Go ahead and score each one as you see fit in the chart above.

Great job! You did it! You identified some Kairos moments from your Chronos journey and rated them in terms of processing potential. The higher scores indicate the impact of the Kairos on your internal reality, which means it's likely to yield more in terms of learning, insight and wisdom. As we'll see, we all have too many Kairos moments each day to process all of them. This scoring system can help you determine which ones are most important to process.

With a bit of practice, you'll find yourself recognizing Kairos moments throughout every day of your life. I will often write some of the more impactful ones on a Post-it Note so I can decide which ones deserve my attention when I have time to process them.

Now, this may be your first experience identifying Kairos moments, so give yourself a pat on the back for doing the work. At this point it's not about being an expert, but about the benefit of simply practicing and familiarizing yourself with a new skill.

During our normal coaching process, we ask our clients to do this exercise on a regular basis and share their Kairos moments with the group. I encourage you to find someone you can share these with and ask them to do the same in return. Remember, we're not at the point of processing these Kairos moments—that comes next.

> Remember, a Kairos moment can be big, small, positive or negative. Let me share a note about positive Kairos moments. They have as much to teach us as any other Kairos, but we often pass them over because we tend to focus on our negative experiences. Positive Kairos moments teach us what we did well, what we may want to repeat or reproduce and serve as bits of wisdom for future situations. As we continue our journey toward processing Kairos moments, don't forget the positive ones. They are goldmines of wisdom and help us sustain desired trajectories.

In the next chapters we'll look at how to mine out the wisdom from these Kairos moments!

REFLECTIVE QUESTIONS

1. On a scale of 1–10, how easy is it for you to identify Kairos moments from your life?

2. Do you have any current, intentional methods for processing your Kairos moments?

3. Identify 2–3 examples from your past where you processed an important event in your life. What did you do? Did you process these moments with anyone? What did you learn?

4. Do you think having a simple tool to process these past events would have helped you in any way? How so?

05

OBSERVE

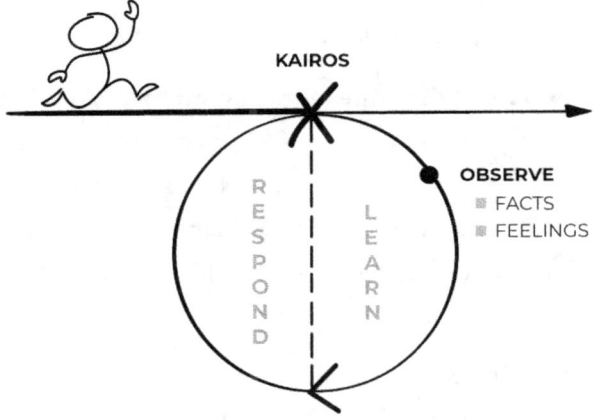

We begin the excavation process by observing *what* happened in our Kairos. If a Kairos is any experience that grabbed our attention, then there's a story that goes with it. Here, we learn to ask the simple question: <u>what happened</u>? We need to recount the story of our Kairos moment, to paint a picture that will help us understand two primary realities: the Facts and our Feelings. Our desire in observing the events of our Kairos is to get as much clarity as possible about the event(s) as they unfolded.

FACTS – We should recount the events to the best of our ability, focusing on the observables. Think of it as painting a picture of what you experienced, removing any interpretation or analysis from the account. It is important to be as objective as possible when observing the facts.

Another way to think of it is like walking into a pitch-dark room and turning the lights on. The light simply exposes what's inside the room but makes no judgment of its contents. Making good observations is a way of shining a light on your experience to determine the contents of your Kairos. You might also think of it like what you'd find in a video recording or a photo.

FEELINGS – Feelings are facts. I know, that may sound odd to some, but let me assure you that feelings are as much facts as the chair you sit in, the car you drive in or the book you're reading (or listening to) right now. Too often, we have dismissed the feelings associated with our Kairos moments as illegitimate, subjective and even irrelevant to engaging a Kairos moment.

It's unhelpful when someone says, "This isn't personal," or "You're being emotional," or "Leave your feelings at the door." Feelings can cloud our judgment (interpretation) of the Kairos, but they are part of the facts of our experience. We cannot control the initial feelings that arise in any Kairos moment. It does us no good to ignore them or dismiss them as they can tell us much about our experience. We are responsible for how we respond to our emotions, but we cannot control the emotions that arise in a Kairos. *Listen up, if we don't own our feelings, they will own us.*

Listen up, if we don't own our feelings, **they will own us.**

Therefore, let's count our feelings in any Kairos as evidence of our experience, to be registered for later interpretation.

Strong emotions can serve as indicators alerting us to a Kairos moment and they can also tell us much about how we're experiencing these moments. We will have to unpack the emotions that both signaled the Kairos as well as those emotions percolating after the fact. In both cases, our feelings serve as evidence that will later help us understand what's going on at a deeper level within ourselves.

Beginning with observations is critical because our brains are like super-computers. We have the ability to compute lots of data and make interpretations at lightning-fast speed. The problem lies in our ability to overlook facts, fill in the ones that are missing and even distort our experiences in the favor of our preconceived biases or desired outcomes. In any Kairos, we are mentally, emotionally and physically impacted. Therefore, we are wise to assume our ability to make objective observations may be impaired by intense emotions.

We've all been in an argument where both parties are recounting the event with very different observations. At first, we might think the other party is lying or twisting the facts, but what I often find is how quickly our interpretation of what we experienced becomes our facts! Dispassionately observing facts is easier said than done. Holding an objective perspective can be challenging, but one we can grow in over time.

Making good observations of any Kairos is important because we can't learn from what we can't see. In other words, mining the

> **Making good observations of any Kairos is important because we can't learn from what we can't see.**

learning from any experience is dependent on a factual understanding of said experience. For this reason, we are best off when others can help us paint a more accurate picture of what happened. We all have biases and blind spots. Whenever possible, ask others who were present to share their observations associated with your Kairos moment. This will give you a fuller picture of what happened. Simply put, more eyes make for a clearer picture.

For each part of the Kairos Circle, I will offer an example of how I practice each step in relation to my opening story. Then I'll offer you an opportunity to do the same for your own Kairos. It's critical you take time to work through each part of the Kairos Circle to develop your comfort and skill. We'll repeat this rhythm for each step of the Kairos Circle.

OBSERVING MY MARRIAGE KAIROS

In the exact moment my wife confronted me with a possible separation, I was unable to compute the full weight of what she was sharing, nor was I able to make sense of it. My self-protecting mechanisms went into overdrive. I needed some time and space to step back and practice this process.

Observing the facts:

- Kandi was initiating a possible separation.
- Kandi was at her wit's end and felt this was the only option.
- She had brought my excessive drinking to my attention many times before this moment.
- Every time she challenged my drinking, I had a "good reason" why it was helpful for my stress.
- My kids were being deeply affected by my irresponsible attitudes and behaviors.
- I was struggling to sleep well.
- I was behaving erratically.
- I was operating in greater isolation.
- I was easily agitated.
- I suffered multiple anxiety attacks over a one-year period.
- I was gaining weight and clothes were not fitting well any longer.
- I was leaning toward friends who would indulge my drinking habits and pity parties.
- My business partners were expressing concern about my health.

Observing the feelings:

- I felt shocked and terrified at the threat of separation.
- I felt angry at the thought of being responsible for our situation.
- I felt embarrassed by how my children were experiencing me.
- I felt shame by how my various behaviors may be impacting both my family and business.
- I had been feeling elevated levels of stress and anxiety for over a year.
- I had been feeling insecure regarding my various business endeavors.
- I had been feeling exhausted and burned out for many months.

There are many more facts and feelings associated with this Kairos, but I hope these lists provide good examples for you. Now it's your turn!

OBSERVATION EXERCISE

Let's put this tool to practice!

1. Choose one of the Kairos moments you identified in the last chapter and put it in the Kairos line below.

2. In the space provided, list as many observations of your Kairos, focusing on both facts and feelings. (If you struggle to assign emotional language to your feelings, simply Google "wheel of emotions" and pick the ones that best capture the feelings associated with your Kairos.).

***We've also provided Kairos Circle Templates in the appendix for your use.

KAIROS: _____

OBSERVE
- FACTS
- FEELINGS

TIPS FOR PRACTICING OBSERVATION

Some things to remember:

- We all have natural biases and blind spots. Own them where you can.
- The emotional impact of any Kairos may impair our ability to make objective observations. Ask for help.
- Facts are not a judgment, but simply exposing what is.
- Our feelings associated with any Kairos are only indicators that we've been impacted, not an interpretation of the Kairos itself.
- It's helpful to step back from a Kairos moment to gain a more objective perspective on our experience.
- Practice writing your observations down on paper. This takes them out of our heads and allows us to see them more objectively outside of ourselves.

OBSERVE – REFLECTIVE QUESTIONS

1. On a scale of 1-10, how good are you at making objective observations about your Kairos moments?
2. When reflecting on a Kairos moment, what can make it difficult for you to make objective observations?
3. Do you find it difficult to accept your feelings in a Kairos as facts? Why so?
4. How comfortable are you asking others to check your observations of a Kairos?
5. Can you accept the impact of a Kairos may impair your ability to practice objective observations? Why or why not?

06

INTERPRET

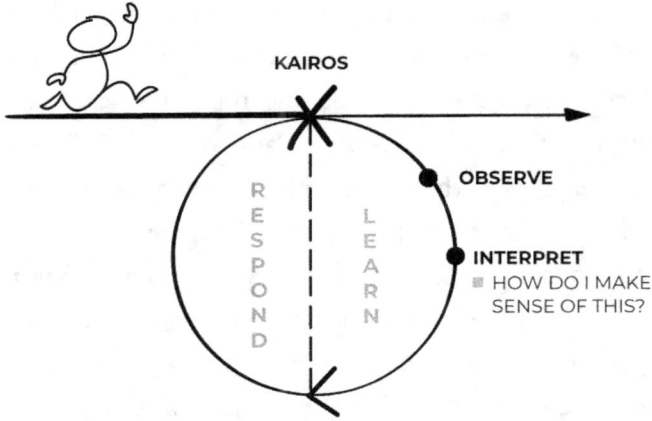

After we've done our best to make observations (ideally with the help of others), we are ready to move on to interpreting our observations. If observing is the process of asking the "what" question, then interpreting our Kairos is asking the "why" question. This is how we look beneath the surface of our Kairos.

Here are some helpful questions to help you dig a bit deeper:

- Why did this happen?
- Why am I affected by this experience?

- Why did I say, do or respond to that experience the way I did?
- Why did they say, do or respond the way they did?
- Why did this situation unfold the way it did?
- How can I make sense of this event?
- Why do I feel the way I feel?

It's important to understand that through our lives we have all developed interpretive lenses or narratives that help us make sense of our life experiences. From our earliest years we learned to interpret our parents' words and tone of voice. We learned to interpret whether "no" really meant "no" or just "maybe." We had to interpret whether other children at school were friends or foes, whether that child liked us, and even how we measured up in our friendship circles. *Was that sarcasm meant to harm or was it just playful? Is that person honking at me trying to say "hi" or are they upset with me?* Whether we realize it or not, we are interpreting every experience in order to determine if it is a threat or an opportunity.

It can get a bit confusing when we remember that two people might interpret the same experience in two very different ways. The same experience may solicit exhilaration in one while dread in another. Why? It's determined by how each interprets the situation. Being asked to speak in front of a crowd may excite one person. They see it as an opportunity to share their perspective, educate the group and even lobby their opinion. For another, it may be seen as a threat as they believe it will expose their own inadequacy as a communicator and cause humiliation. Either way, our interpretations reflect our subjective assessments of the observable realities.

Consider issues of conflict. Some interpret conflict as an opportunity to learn from other views while sharpening their own. They value open communication and a chance for win-win solutions. But for another, conflict may only represent the inevitability of harsh debate, argumentation and win-lose warfare.

The point I'm making is that if multiple people can interpret the same experience in different ways, then we would do well to remember that our interpretation may not always be the most accurate one.

OBSTACLE OR OPPORTUNITY?

A helpful way to assess the health of our interpretations is to determine whether we see the Kairos as an obstacle or opportunity. When we see a Kairos as an obstacle, it's usually because we're feeling threatened, which often means we're in a self-protecting posture. This is often a sign we're interpreting the Kairos as happening *to* us, instead of *for* us. When in a defensive posture, our ability to read the situation accurately diminishes because our first priority is survival. Biologically, when threatened, our amygdala (emotional thinking) kicks in, shutting down our prefrontal cortex (rational thinking), and we usually default to fight-or-flight behaviors. Either way, in this posture, our only concern is to escape or eliminate the threat. Operating from fear or insecurity often robs us of the opportunity to learn from the Kairos.

I will concede that when facing a tiger in the jungle or an armed robber, our amygdala serves us well to defend or escape. In these instances, fighting or fleeing may be the best response. The problem is how easily we begin to see co-workers, family and fellow freeway travelers as tigers and assailants!

A helpful way to assess the health of our interpretations is to make a list of how we see the Kairos - is it an obstacle or opportunity? Do we see this Kairos happening *to* us or *for* us? If we see the Kairos as an obstacle or threat, then we would do well to slow down and reconsider our interpretive lens. If, on the other hand, we see it as an opportunity (happening *for* us), then we are positioned to learn something about ourselves and the environment. In this case, we can trust that our perspective is likely sober and helpful.

Any Kairos that feels threatening can be reframed as an opportunity. For example, when confronted by my wife with a possible separation, I was eventually able to reframe the situation. Where I first interpreted her words as an obstacle to our future, I was able to reframe the situation as an opportunity to take personal responsibility and grow. This was an opportunity! Instead of focusing on my wife's position (something I can't control), I reframed it into an opportunity to become a better version of myself (something I can control).

Below is a simple table on which to list your interpretations about any Kairos. Take the Kairos you've been working with from the earlier chapters and reflect on how you view it. Consider how you might see the Kairos as an obstacle or opportunity and why. Do you see it happening *to* you or *for* you? It's natural to have some in both columns.

OBSTACLE OR OPPORTUNITY?

KAIROS	OBSTACLE (happening to you) WHY?	OPPORTUNITY (happening for you) WHY?

I believe every Kairos, challenging as it may be, is an opportunity to learn about ourselves, others and the situation we're exploring. Every Kairos acts like a mirror, reflecting back to us our attitudes and behaviors as well as the interpretive lenses we use to make sense of our experiences. In our youth we developed interpretive lenses largely from survival instincts and the influence of those who shaped how we see the world. As adults, our interpretive lenses deserve a thorough examination to determine whether they still serve us effectively.

Have you ever been in a situation when your past experiences are negatively impacting your current perspective? Of course. We all have. This is an example of how an interpretive lens developed from past experience can undermine our ability to make clear, healthy decisions in the present. In some cases, we feel enslaved to the paradigms we've either inherited or adopted through dysfunctional relationships and painful experiences. Here's the good news: as adults we get to choose our interpretive lenses. This is part of our superpower.

I grew up on the edge of a city border where our docile community was only a hundred yards away from a drug and gang-ridden neighborhood. Both neighborhoods shared parks and schools, so our paths crossed often. I have vivid memories of being chased by kids from the other neighborhood and being bullied in school, so I developed a general fear about getting beat up. It was years later when I realized how much these experiences shaped my interpretation of safety in the world. I found myself intensely cautious while walking about in major downtown areas. I was constantly checking my environment while riding a subway. I was even irrationally suspicious of Uber and Taxi drivers.

From my childhood experiences, I had developed an interpretive lens that saw the world as unsafe, where people were out to get me and could not be trusted. As an adult, I was making unhelpful decisions rooted in past experiences. I knew these interpretive lenses were unhelpful, but I felt beholden to them, stuck in the past. How could I be free from them? What new interpretive lenses would serve me better?

This tool isn't just about solving problems, making decisions and recovering our mental and emotional sobriety. **This tool helps us transform the narratives we live from.**

Take a moment and see if you can identify in your life where a past experience is negatively impacting your present decisions. Consider what interpretive lens you developed from your past and what a more empowering lens might be.

THE GREAT EXCHANGE

This may be the most important thing I'm going to say to you in the entire book: *this tool isn't just about solving problems, making decisions and recovering our mental and emotional sobriety. This tool helps us transform the narratives we live from.* Without going too deep into the psychological explanation, it's helpful to understand that since we were young, each of us has been developing our narratives. The stories we tell ourselves help us make sense of our life experiences. They have shaped the way we see ourselves, our environment and how we engage every moment of our lives.

Here's some really good news. No matter your past, no matter what narratives you inherited or adopted in your earlier years, *you get to choose the narratives you live with today*! We spend lots of time and money with counselors to do this very thing. They try to help us confront our past, reconcile our experiences and exchange unhelpful narratives for helpful ones.

I'm not saying we get to change whether we grew up in wealth or poverty, health or abuse, or even the education we received early on. However, these experiences did shape our narrative. The stories we tell ourselves are the tapes playing in our minds that determine how we interpret the present. If we were often picked last for a team, then the narrative we might tell ourselves is that we're not worth being picked for anything, no one wants us on their team, or that we're not good enough. This might inhibit our willingness to apply for a promotion, pursue a larger client or go on a date with someone we've convinced ourselves is out of our league.

Perhaps we've had a track record of failed romantic relationships and now live with the narrative that we're just not cut out for long-term relationships, so we live with the limiting belief that we'll never find love. Some have referred to these limiting beliefs as "self-fulfilling prophecies." We believe something to be true, therefore we act in accordance with those expectations. Simply put, the stories we tell ourselves (for better or worse) shape what we believe about ourselves and others. Moreover, they affect the decisions we make every day.

> We may not get to choose our past, but we do get to choose who we want to be now and the narratives we move forward with. You and I can choose our narratives!

We can reframe our experiences to discover the gold in even our most difficult stories. We can choose the version of ourselves we want to move forward with. We can identify *why* we are interpreting an experience in a particular way and *choose* to exchange an old, unhelpful narrative for a new, more helpful one. We call this "The Great Exchange." Whenever we discover that we're operating with an unhelpful interpretive lens, we get to exchange it for one that helps us understand our experience with greater clarity. This liberates us to see any life experience as happening *for* us rather that *to* us.

We may not be in control of the world around us, but we are responsible for how we make sense of it. Let's go a bit deeper.

Often times a difficult Kairos will put us under pressure and we may interpret it as a threat. Our temptation may be to assume a victim mentality where we believe the Kairos is happening *to* us. We feel we have no control and default to a victim mindset, believing the world is against us and our only option is to retreat or defend ourselves against the onslaught of unwanted circumstances. Another default may be toward a villain mindset. This often happens when we feel our only recourse to unwanted experiences is to impose our will and control our environment. Either way, these interpretive lenses distort our view and understanding of ourselves, others and the world we experience, making it almost impossible to respond well.

What are our alternatives?

We can upgrade our interpretive lenses by identifying the lies or limiting beliefs that flow from a distorted narrative for a lens rooted in truth or empowering beliefs. Let me illustrate with a real conversation from a coaching call. Sally makes a mistake in a report, which is only realized during a team meeting. Sally has interpreted from past experiences that her mistakes will cause others to see her as inadequate and unworthy of her place on the team. This is her narrative. She shrinks back and withdraws from contributing further in the meeting. Later, while on her drive home, she berates herself aloud, "You're so stupid! The team now thinks you're a joke.

You should just shut up and let others do all the talking." How Sally interprets her experience determines what she believes about herself, especially how she thinks others see her. Her interpretation drives a personal narrative of self-doubt, and shame. All of this leads her to withdrawal. This narrative drives an action that is rooted in a distorted view of herself. Her limiting beliefs are now undermining her ability to contribute her best self.

Take a moment to reflect on this scenario. Ask yourself:

- What lies or limiting beliefs is Sally holding on to?
- What truths or empowering beliefs might set Sally free to see herself more clearly so she can bring her full self to the next meeting?
- Where do you connect with Sally's story? Can you identify any limiting beliefs that impact how you show up at home or work?

Now, imagine while Sally is driving home she instead thinks to herself, "I'm sad I made a significant error in the report. Making a mistake does not mean I'm a mistake. I'll learn from this, grow and do better next time. I'm an important member of my team and need to keep showing up!" That's the kind of self-talk reflecting empowering beliefs that will help Sally continue bringing the best version of herself to work. This is an example of what we'll later learn as self-coaching. And I believe the best leaders are self-coaching leaders.

Here's the good news about the freedom available in every Kairos. We get to choose our narratives, the beliefs we operate from. In other words, we get to choose the stories we tell ourselves that empower the best version of ourselves as opposed to

> **I believe the best leaders are self-coaching leaders.**

a diminished, prejudiced one. Our work with leaders often entails helping them expose false narratives and exchanging them for ones that reveal a greater truth about who they are and who they are becoming. These narratives rooted in truth empower them to behave more consistently with their core values and move toward the best version of themselves.

INTERPRETING MY MARRIAGE KAIROS

- Excessive drinking wasn't helping me, but actually creating added stress and compounding the feelings of depression.
- My wife's initiation of a separation wasn't because she didn't love me, but because she did and wanted my best.
- Not dealing with my stress in constructive ways led me to isolate and withdraw from family and friends. These were the people I needed most in distress.
- My physical health was emblematic of my internal struggles for self-control and peace.
- I had behaved poorly over a period of time, but that didn't mean I was a bad person.
- I had experienced difficult times in the past and made it through as a better version of myself. This situation, regardless of the consequences, could be the same if reframed as an opportunity.

INTERPRETATION EXERCISE

Continue processing your Kairos from the last chapter by using the space below to list your interpretations of your Kairos moment. Reflect on whether you see each one as an obstacle or opportunity. Do your best to identify the narratives at work in your interpretations and scrutinize whether they are helpful using the questions in the box below.

- Does this narrative reflect the facts?
- Does this narrative reflect what is true about myself?
- Does this narrative represent who I want to be?
- Does this narrative represent who I am in my best moments?
- Does this narrative represent the best version of myself?
- Do my closest friends agree with this narrative?
- Does this narrative breathe life or death into me?
- Does this narrative cause me to see others/circumstances as an opportunity or obstacle?
- Does this narrative cause me to see situations with hope or fear?
- Would I recommend others to adopt this narrative for themselves?
- Is my narrative for or against myself/others/circumstances?
- Does this narrative cause me to treat myself/others/situation with honor, dignity, respect, kindness, belief?
- Does this narrative serve or betray myself/others?

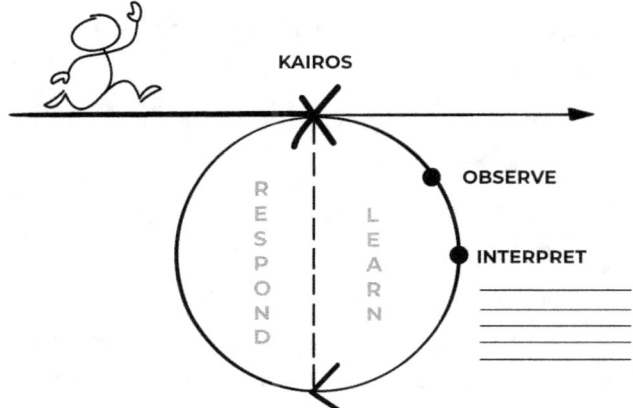

TIPS FOR PRACTICING INTERPRETATION

- **EXAMINE:** We must examine our internal attitudes, ruthlessly evaluating them to expose false narratives and exchange them for more empowering ones. This is an opportunity to expose limiting beliefs that undermine our sense of self and ability to engage life with clarity and confidence. We get to choose what we believe about ourselves! Don't let your past do this for you!

- **IDENTIFY:** Identifying lies we've been trapped in for years can be difficult and even scary. We may find these false narratives have become so familiar we mistake them for who we are. We must differentiate between our false narratives and our true identity. Narratives are only as good as they help us operate from our desired self.

- **UTILIZE OTHERS:** Whether with a counselor or a trusted friend, we often need help to practice the Great Exchange. Others can help us identify deeply rooted limiting beliefs. They can also help us consider what new beliefs about ourselves and the world may be more empowering.

INTERPRET – REFLECTIVE QUESTIONS

1. How comfortable are you reflecting on, and interpreting your Kairos moments?

2. What are the Kairos moments where you find yourself jumping to conclusions, making assumptions or operating from a negativity bias?

3. Do you have any trusted friends or partners who help you process and interpret your Kairos moments?

4. Identify one example where you have made a Great Exchange in your thinking? What was it and how did you make that trade?

5. Identify one narrative you often turn to you know isn't helpful to you—if you could, what would you exchange it for?

6. What's one narrative you operate with that helps you operate as the best version of yourself?

07

DISCOVER

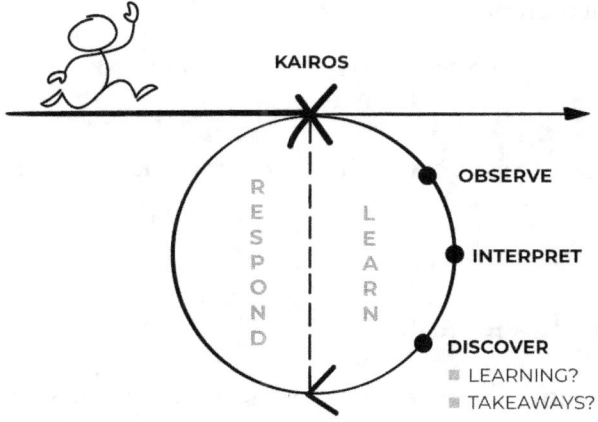

The process of excavating our internal narratives, which drive our attitudes and behaviors, can be messy, disorientating, even unnerving. But exchanging distortions for truth will lead to increased freedom and peace. This peace comes from realizing we, rather than our circumstances, have the authority to determine *who we are* and how we will lead our lives. The next step in the Kairos Circle is to discover what we're learning by identifying and clarifying our takeaways. This is how we mine out wisdom!

The process of Discovery is asking:

- What am I learning about myself, others, or my situation from this Kairos?
- What are my takeaways?
- What new narrative will lead to greater freedom and empowerment?
- Who am I regardless of the situation (reaffirming our helpful narrative)?
- What is the best version of me I want to move forward with?
- What insight have I discovered that may serve me in the future?

WHAT ARE WE LEARNING?

It is imperative we remember the primary question we're asking in the first half of the Kairos Circle - What are we learning? Every Kairos is a goldmine of discovery. It's not uncommon for people to have a powerful Kairos, process it a bit and then walk away empty-handed! Why? Because they did not excavate the learning available. That's like panning for gold, seeing some glittering pieces in your tray, and then dumping it back into the river. One of the primary purposes of processing any Kairos is to pull out the learning and insights, otherwise we'll have done a lot of work with no reward. The way we can ensure we've excavated the value from the Kairos is to ask the above questions until clarity emerges. Similar to making observations, we will benefit from inviting someone else to help us process our Kairos and identify our key takeaways.

Let's start with some simple discovery questions we can begin with for every Kairos at this point:

1. What am I learning about myself?
2. What am I learning about others?
3. What am I learning about my circumstances?

WHAT AM I LEARNING ABOUT MYSELF? Wisdom begins with the practice of self-awareness. Every Kairos, even if triggered by someone else, is an opportunity to discover greater insights about ourselves. Why did we get upset? Why did we respond so strongly? Why were we triggered? These are the kinds of questions that we start with during the interpretation step that teach us something about ourselves. This is vital learning.

Understanding what triggers, excites, annoys, encourages, frustrates, irritates, threatens and empowers us matters. Why? So we can lead ourselves more effectively. Too often, in Kairos moments we're preoccupied with understanding everything else but ourselves. They say, "Beauty is in the eye of the beholder." I say *everything* is in the eye of the beholder! Our view of reality is shaped by our interpretive lenses, so understanding ourselves and how we view things is paramount.

Examples of what I may learn about myself:

- I am easily agitated when others are late to meetings.
- I am motivated by words of encouragement.

- When I'm stressed, I find it difficult to listen well in conversations.
- I have more energy throughout the day when I exercise first thing in the morning.
- I do better when I don't have multiple back-to-back meetings.

Take a moment and identify one or two things you've learned about yourself recently.

WHAT AM I LEARNING ABOUT OTHERS? Another great benefit of processing a Kairos is the opportunity to learn something new about the people around us. Through the process of observation and interpretation we may discover new facts, insights or perspectives about others that give us a chance to engage them with greater clarity. Perhaps we discover someone is less trustworthy than we previously understood or maybe we discover our colleague is a far better friend than we thought. Either way, every Kairos offers us a chance to learn more about the people we engage with.

> Seeing others more clearly allows us to lead them more effectively.

Recently, while I was working with a team via video conference, I noticed that the body language of a particular individual communicated disinterest or aloofness. When I asked their team leader about this individual's appearance during calls, the leader let me know that individual was loving the coaching process but is stoic and still developing their nonverbal communication skills. It would have been easy for me to interpret this individual through a negative lens. I learned something about that individual by processing my Kairos that will change how I view and treat that individual.

Examples of what I may learn about others:

- Body language is not always the best indicator of what someone is thinking or feeling.
- My teenage son is not disinterested in our family conversation; he's still thinking about his soccer game.
- My client is not avoiding me but has been slammed with new business.

WHAT AM I LEARNING ABOUT MY CIRCUMSTANCES? Kairos moments will often reveal a deeper understanding of our environment or circumstances. Recently, while traveling on the freeway I found myself deeply annoyed with the driver in front of me who was traveling far too slow for the fast lane. I flashed my high beams, rode their coattails and even gave them a gentle honk, but to no avail. After what seemed like an eternity, they eventually moved aside and that's when I realized there was a highway patrol car in front of them! Needless to say, we sometimes find the circumstances of a Kairos have more to teach us about our experience than the people involved in it.

Examples of what I may learn from Kairos circumstances:

- The person I thought was blocking the fast lane was really stuck behind a highway patrol car.

- I thought my wife was mad at me when I arrived home only to discover she was frustrated with our dog soiling the carpet.

- I thought our most loyal client was unhappy because they did not increase their contract the following year, only to learn they were being sued and needed to allocate resources for that battle.

- I thought I was unable to write a part of this book, but it was just that a busy coffee shop with lots of noise was not an ideal writing environment.

TAKEAWAYS – PUTTING YOUR LEARNING TO WORDS

At this point, when working with clients, we ask them to verbalize to the best of their ability what they are learning through *takeaways*. This is our language to ensure we can convert our learning from insight into action. To do this, we're going to practice putting our learning to spoken or written words. The articulation process helps us take ownership of what we're learning. It gives us a chance to check our takeaways with others and verify our perspective is rooted in empowering beliefs. This process cements the new learning as part of our new narrative and gives us the best chance of living into a new reality.

TAKE OWNERSHIP - Learning is not something others can give us. They can make suggestions or offer their perspective, but it's important that we fully own any learning that comes out of our Kairos. This is part of taking 100% responsibility for our Kairos journey. If we don't fully own our learning and takeaways, then we cannot confidently respond to them. For this reason, it's OK to take time to process your learning and takeaways. Don't let others rush you to respond to a Kairos until you have clarified and are confident in what you've learned.

GET OUTSIDE PERSPECTIVE - It can be very helpful to get an outside perspective on our Kairos by inviting trusted friends, coworkers or counselors. They can reflect back to us what they are hearing and even offer their own suggested takeaways. As long as they are serving us and not imposing, they can provide for us a constructive space to process our thoughts until we are ready to land on our takeaways. They might also help us identify any blind spots, unhelpful narratives or gaps in our thinking. I will very often invite my wife, business partner, older brother or counselor to help me process a larger Kairos to check my honesty and perspective. They can help me map my Kairos around the Circle to ensure I don't get stuck or give up. I'll even invite them into smaller Kairos moments just to confirm I'm on the right track.

CEMENT YOUR LEARNING - Science has long understood the impact of our words on our thinking. Simply put, what we declare aloud either reinforces or disrupts our internal thought patterns. By declaring, out loud, what we're learning (or even writing it in a journal), we establish and reinforce our key takeaways from any Kairos. Have you ever been reading a book, had a powerful insight and then forgot it a few minutes later? That's probably because you didn't share it with anyone or write it down. Sharing our learning with others, or writing it down, goes a long way to cementing these bits of wisdom in our minds and shifts our internal reality. Changing our internal reality precipitates any external changes that will follow.

TAKEAWAYS FROM MY MARRIAGE KAIROS

- There was hope for my marriage if my wife could see me engage a deep and meaningful process of personal transformation, beginning with my excessive drinking.
- I desperately wanted to be the best version of myself for my wife, kids, friends and team.
- Alcohol was robbing me of my health and needed to be dealt with.
- I needed a constructive pathway to deal with stress and depression.
- I needed to take responsibility and reconcile with anyone who was adversely affected by my poor attitudes and behaviors.
- I had the rest of my life ahead of me and wanted to pursue a new trajectory!

DISCOVER EXERCISE

It's your turn! In the space below take some time to list the learning, insights, wisdom and takeaways from your Kairos. Remember, practice makes better, so do your best and share with a trusted friend to get their input.

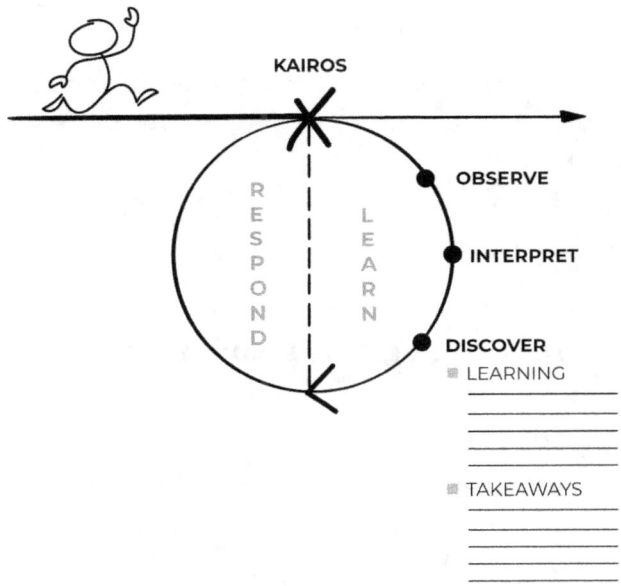

TIPS FOR PRACTICING DISCOVERY

Some things to remember:

- A takeaway is any insight, learning, piece of wisdom or mindset shift you believe helps you practice the best version of yourself.
- Healthy takeaways are always in the best interest of all parties involved in the Kairos.
- We benefit by checking our takeaways with others to ensure they are reflective of positive, empowering narratives.
- Takeaways very often serve as bits of wisdom we can apply in future situations.

DISCOVER — REFLECTIVE QUESTIONS

1. Do you find it easy or difficult to articulate takeaways from life experiences? Why do you think that is?
2. Do you have trusted friends or partners you can invite to help you mine out the takeaways from your Kairos moments?
3. Identify one key takeaway you have gleaned from your life over the past year.
4. Identify one takeaway from your past that you still apply today?

08

PLAN

As we put language to our learning, we are ready to cultivate growth through an intentional response. But first, let me prepare us for the transition as we go from Discover to Plan, and then on to Transformation. *Revelation is not the same thing as transformation.* Learning something cognitively will only lead to genuine transformation when we put it to action. It's not enough to discover truth. We must plant it, water it and nurture its growth. We must move from increasing our self-awareness to proactively leading ourselves into new behaviors. New behaviors are how we cultivate our new truths, attitudes and narratives.

This happens when we move from the question, "What am I learning" to "How am I going to respond?"

In the Hellenistic culture of old (think ancient Greek culture), they believed they could think their way into new behaviors. This was a culture deeply rooted in the discipline of philosophy, from which later the famous words were born, "I think, therefore I am."[5]

---

5   René Descartes; *Discourse on the Method*, 1637

They held to the notion that by cognitively understanding their world and putting language to it, a transformed life would follow. In a sense, they believed that new thinking led to new behaviors. Our current, western culture is largely born out of this philosophical approach to life. We tend to value good ideas, even when disconnected from transformed outcomes.

Let me be clear—I have argued previously about the importance of developing empowering narratives. This implies sober and accurate thinking. I'm not discounting the importance of good thinking, but rather suggesting that good thinking alone is not enough. We need good thinking that is cultivated through intentional behaviors. We've all had thoughts or convictions that never amounted to much. Consider New Year's resolutions as an example. We have a thought, decide we want a different life, only to discover days, weeks or months later we've not changed much. Why? Because we cannot think our way into new behaviors.

Instead, I invite us to consider a different approach. I believe through intentional and practiced behaviors, we cultivate new ways of thinking. I won't get into the brain science behind what I'm saying, but I assure you this is real. Our thinking is intimately tied to our attitudes and behaviors; and of the two, it is our behaviors that are more impactful upon our thinking than the other way around. For this reason, I often share with clients that our behaviors often betray what we *think* we think!

Our attitudes and behaviors will often reveal the prevailing thoughts and attitudes we carry. That's a sobering thought! We may think we want to lose weight, but our actions will reveal what our greatest desires are. We may think we want peace in a relationship, but our actions often reveal our true mindset.

Years ago, a former employer called me into their office to confront my behaviors with the team I was leading. After listening to her concerns, I said that she didn't know what was in my heart, and that I didn't intend to come across the way others were experiencing me. I blamed them for not understanding my intent. She replied with something I'll never forget. "Eric," she said, "I don't know what's in your heart and I'm not second-guessing your intent. You are evaluated on the basis of your behaviors, nothing more and nothing less." This began my understanding that my actions will, more often than not, betray what I think my true intentions are.

Whenever our intentions do not align with how others experience us, it is possible we've been misunderstood. But it's more likely that we're unaware of how our behaviors are impacting others. It's in our best interest to take responsibility and reflect on what others are saying of us. It doesn't mean they're right, but we win when we take every opportunity to grow.

I've watched my wife produce incredible vegetables in our garden over many seasons. I will often look at the small packages the even smaller seeds come in. On the cover of the package is an amazing picture of what could be, but the seeds themselves are often terribly unimpressive. I often think there's no way these big, beautiful vegetables can come from a tiny seed. New thinking is like the picture on the cover. It's beautiful and promises much, but the real work is in preparing the soil, planting the seed, regularly tending to the moisture and sunlight, warding off pests and persevering until something finally pops through the surface. Even then, it can take a while before we have much to show for. In other words, *new thinking must be cultivated through regular behaviors until we have a new garden of attitudes and actions that are more consistent with who we say we want to be.*

New thinking must be cultivated through regular behaviors until we have a new garden of attitudes and actions that are more consistent with who we say we want to be.

Personal transformation must begin with learning from our life experiences, then determining the best way to respond for all parties involved. We are now ready to move into the second half of the Kairos Circle, beginning with making a plan.

PLANNING YOUR TRANSFORMATION

This is the part of the Kairos Circle where we get to put "our money where our mouth is," so to speak. As I've said, the change process doesn't take hold until we act on our learning. Here are some of the benefits we can expect as we respond to our learning with good plans:

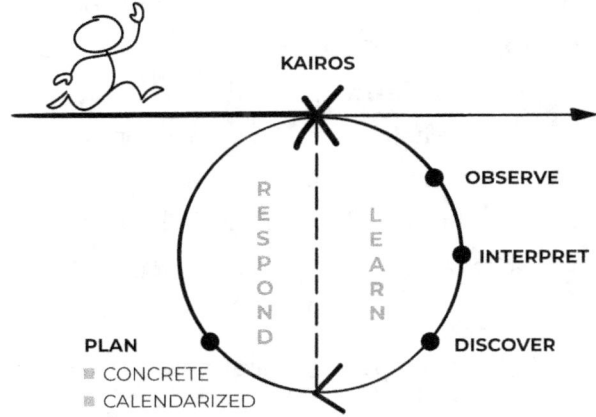

- We will put the best version of ourselves back in the driver's seat.
- We will integrate our behaviors with our desired narrative.
- We will lead through action.

Making a plan for how we'll respond to our learning is the first step toward putting the wisdom we've acquired into action. This is us moving from the world of good ideas to "boots-on-the-ground" practical responses. Remember, this is how we successfully integrate our learning into any situation in which we find ourselves. In this section we'll focus on how every good plan must be both, Concrete and Calendarized.

CONCRETE PLAN – A concrete plan is actionable, measurable and accountable.

By actionable, I mean a plan must be something we can act on, something that requires a response from us. How often have we heard someone say, "I need to pick up a new hobby," or "I gotta watch that new movie," or "I have to make a decision on this issue?" These reflect cognitive learning, but these are not plans. They are aspirations. They are hopes, dreams, even visions for life, but they are not going to move the needle. Aspirations are born from experiential insights. But, left in this form, will rarely ever translate into new behaviors. For practical results, we need an actionable plan.

Below is a table comparing aspirational ideas with actionable plans:

ASPIRATIONAL	ACTIONABLE
I need to pick up a new hobby	I will learn how to play the piano, paint with watercolors or join a bicycling group
I gotta watch that new movie	I will find what theater that movie is playing at, which times works best and buy the movie tickets
We ought to vacation more	We will plan a trip for this Spring to Italy (still on my aspirational list!)
I need to get in shape	I will join a gym and hire a personal trainer to help me achieve my fitness goals
I need to finish the rough draft of this book	I will block out the necessary times in my schedule until I finish this rough draft
We should have more sex	We will plan at least one night each week to connect physically
I have to make a decision on this issue	I will invite a trusted friend to process this decision with me to determine the best way forward

You'll notice aspirational statements begin with "I need to," "I gotta," or "I have to." These simply communicate intent, but not necessarily action. You can't be held accountable for an aspiration since it's no different to a wish, a hope or a desire. They're a good start, but not an actionable plan. Actionable language begins with "I will," or "We will." Try saying the statements in the table above out loud and see if you can feel the difference!

Whenever I get to this point in the Kairos Circle with a client (or myself), I pay careful attention to the language used in communicating how they want to move into the future. I then push them (or myself) toward actionable language.

Recently, a client responded to a challenge I gave them with, "I agree, Eric. I need to have a conversation with my board about next year's compensation package." I gently nudged him with, "Don't tell me what you need to do. Tell me what you plan to do." He flashed his patented smirk and retorted, "You're right. I'll put it on the agenda for the next board meeting. Concrete and calendarized, right?" That made me smile.

CALENDARIZED PLAN - A calendarized plan is either a onetime or ongoing scheduled event.

> **Putting your plan on the calendar is like setting an alarm to make sure you wake up to your plan.**

Transformative plans are both concrete and calendarized. Simply put, any plan that does not make your calendar is too easily forgotten or dismissed. Calendarizing your plan will better ensure it actually happens. We're all busy and have lots on our minds, so putting your plan on the calendar is like setting an alarm to make sure you wake up to your plan.

First let's examine the difference between non-calendarized plans versus calendarized.

- Non-calendarized: "I'm going to talk with my spouse and apologize for losing my temper." This is concrete, but not calendarized.

- Calendarized: "I'm going to talk to my spouse tonight when I get home at 6pm (or after dinner at 7:30pm) to apologize for losing my temper." This is calendarized.

Some may balk at the importance of calendarizing a plan. They might say it's childish or pedantic. They may suggest they're adults and don't need this kind of handholding. My response is always the same—if we want to see growth and transformation, then it's worth doing whatever possible to ensure we successfully act on our learning.

There's no shame in planning the things that matter most to us. I have found incredible benefit from planning dates with my spouse and kids, times for regular reflection or meditation and even doing simple chores, like laundry, gassing up my car and doing yard work. Truth is, if it's on my calendar, then I know it's more than an aspirational desire, it's something I am committed to and accountable for.

RECOMMENDATIONS FOR PLAN-MAKING

RETURN ON INVESTMENT (ROI) - We must clarify the results we want from any plan. Clarifying your Return on Investment is essential to make sure your plan is pointing you in the right direction. If we don't clarify what we're fighting for, we'll either lose momentum for lack of vision, or we'll accept subpar results. Determining your ROI will help you strategize a plan that is most likely to give you the intended results.

We have to remember that our plan is not our ROI. Our plan should help us cultivate our ROI. Let me illustrate with a mistake I often made. After a fight with my wife, I would realize that I had overreacted or spoken too harshly with her. I would determine to apologize for my behavior, hoping that would make peace between us. When my apology was met with more expressions of her frustration, I would feel confused, and that my apology was perhaps in vain. Later I learned that I had made my plan the ROI. I thought a simple apology was enough, and it wasn't. Once I clarified that my intended ROI was peace with my wife, I was able to add to my apology a plan to listen and appreciate my wife's frustration and pain.

Making a plan without a clear ROI is like jumping in your car, hitting the road, but with no idea where you're headed. Our plans are only as good as they help us achieve our intended results.

K.I.S.S. - We've all heard the acronym, K.I.S.S. (Keep It Simple Stupid). Our plans should be as simple as possible while giving us the best chance to put our learning into action. We don't need to raise the barriers to action any higher than they already are, so K.I.S.S.! Years ago, a client realized they had a very low degree of leadership literacy. They had taken over a large, successful family business at a young age when their father had passed. They were overwhelmed most of the time with spreadsheets, P & L statements, balance sheets, sales numbers and the like. Who could expect anything else from someone who had been thrown into the deep end prematurely? The problem is that he had little know-how when it came to leading his team, developing department heads, and many other basic leadership skills.

When he brought me his plan, there were at least twenty-five bullet points detailing everything he would read, listen to, or attend in order to practice more effective leadership. I assured him they were all great ideas, but he needed to choose three he felt would move the needle most effectively over the next six months. I deeply appreciated his gusto but was saving him from having to make a future plan to recover from complete burnout! Our plans should serve us, not the other way around.

ONE-TIME VS. ONGOING - It's worth touching on the difference between One-Time Plans vs. Ongoing Plans. Both are equally important, but each one serves different purposes. One-time plans help us engage with any situation that requires a singular response for a particular outcome. On the other hand, ongoing plans are best utilized when we're trying to cultivate new attitudes and behaviors over a longer period of time. For example, if you lose your temper with your spouse, you'll make a one-time plan to apologize to them the next time you're together. You wouldn't necessarily make a plan to apologize every week for that one-time indiscretion. However, if you're trying to lose weight, a one-time plan won't get you very far. For this you'll need an ongoing plan for exercise, new dietary habits and maybe even a season working with a personal trainer or health coach.

RECALIBRATING PLANS - From time to time we will discover that our plan is not working. Sometimes we will discover the current plan just needs a little tweaking. Other times we'll realize our plan was never going to yield the intended result. Either way, this is normal. Don't be afraid to review the efficacy of your plan and recalibrate until you find the plan that works best. I have found the more I practice making plans and inviting others to help, the more proficient I become. We'll talk more about this in the chapter on practice.

PLAN FOR MY MARRIAGE KAIROS

(Each of these were calendarized at the time)

- I will engage personal counseling to help sort through ongoing stress and anxiety, to determine deeper reasons for depression and to develop healthier coping mechanisms (ongoing plan).
- I will meet with my family to take 100% personal responsibility and apologize for the impact of my attitudes and behaviors on them. I will also share my plan for recovery, healing and a healthier future (one-time plan).
- I will share with those friends and team members I spend the most time with of my plan to cut drinking out as part of my normal lifestyle and a regular check-in schedule to help me stay on track (one-time and ongoing plan).

PLAN – EXERCISE

Take time to convert your takeaways from the last chapter into concrete and calendarized plans. Again, you will benefit from processing these with a trusted partner to ensure your plan(s) have the best chance of yielding the intended results.

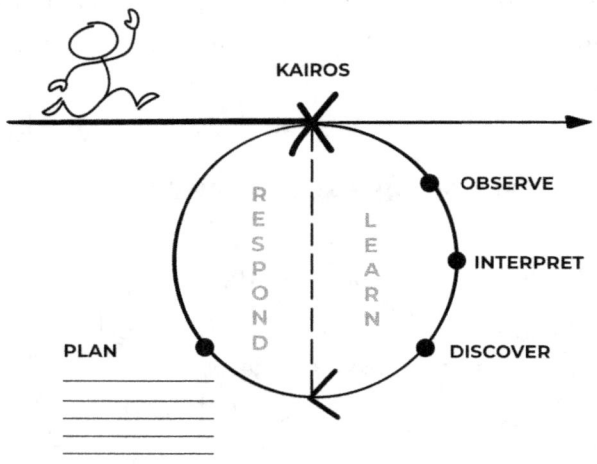

TIPS FOR PRACTICING PLANNING

- Determine your ROI
- Remember to K.I.S.S
- Determine what will be one-time vs ongoing plans
- Recalibrate your plan as needed

PLAN – REFLECTIVE QUESTIONS

1. Is making a Concrete and Calendarized plan a strength or a weakness of mine?
2. Do I have a difficult time following through on plans?
3. Do I find myself secretly resenting the plans I make?
4. Would I benefit from asking others to help me create plans?
5. What is one example of a plan I've made but didn't follow through with?
6. Are there areas of my life/leadership that I want to change but have struggled to make or keep a plan?

09
PARTNER

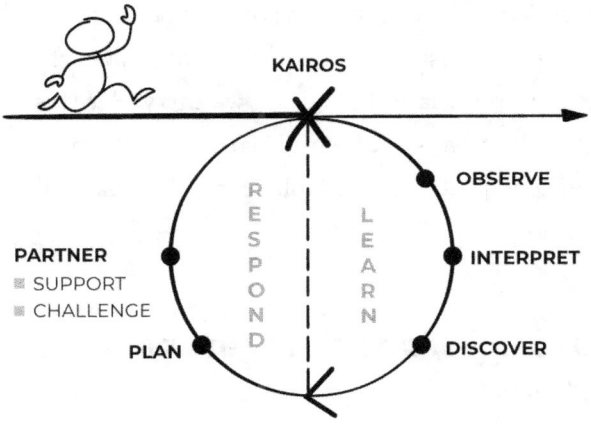

Acting on plans and making personal changes is hard work! We can grow weary, become discouraged and even find our plans may not be serving us the way we had hoped. We need as much help as we can get, therefore the next step in the Kairos Circle is to secure partnership for our journey.

The purpose of having a Kairos Partner cannot be overstated. First, we are more likely to squeeze the learning from any Kairos moment with help from another's perspective. Second, our plans stand a better chance of being both concrete and calendarized if someone else is checking it for these qualities. Third, in the process of engaging our plans we may grow frustrated, tired, impatient or even tempted to eschew our plan. We need encouragement! There's an old Hebrew saying, "Two are better than one." In life, we stand a better chance of succeeding in anything when we have the right kind of partnership!

Before we jump into some practical handles for partnership, let me address something I see many leaders unaware of - leadership is a lonely endeavor. The higher we go on the totem pole, the more rarified the space. It is very difficult for those down chain to fully understand or appreciate the burden we carry. For this reason, it is imperative that we seek helpful partners for our journey. We need outside perspective and people to lean on. Leadership is hard. Don't do it alone!

WHAT KIND OF KAIROS PARTNER ARE WE LOOKING FOR?

PARTNERSHIP VS. POLICING – First, partnership is not a form of policing. We don't need others looking over our shoulders, waiting to catch us in failure. As adults we don't need anyone parenting us or lording their position over us. We're looking for partners who understand their role is to help us process, learn, plan and fight for any plan that comes out of a Kairos. They are our comrades in arms, the Goose to our Maverick, the Samwise to our Frodo (Yes, I'm dating myself!).

I recently received a text from a friend who wanted to grab a phone call and follow up on a previous conversation where he noticed I didn't have any clear health goals. We've done this for one another over the years. However, upon receiving this text I immediately felt anxiety about the conversation. I knew I wasn't clear about my health goals and felt some shame since I had spent years supporting and challenging him toward the same. I jumped on the call anyway and was relieved by his posture and tone through our conversation. He reminded me that we partner one another, because we care for, and love each other. I shared that I was struggling to determine particular goals and invited his help to process what goals might be helpful for me. When the conversation ended, I was flooded with a sense of gratitude for having this kind of partnership in my life, to help me grow and develop in the areas that matter most to me.

SUPPORT & CHALLENGE – The key to creating an empowering relationship or culture is understanding the importance of providing both support and challenge. We need our Kairos Partners to support us through encouragement and empathy. We need them to listen, give us perspective and helpful resources.

We also need them to challenge us by helping us be accountable to our plan, holding our feet to the fire, pushing us to move beyond our comfort zone and staying the course.

Without helpful support, we're sure to become discouraged, frustrated and fall off our plan. Without helpful challenge, we're likely to default to what feels most comfortable, take the path of least resistance and fall short of our intended results.

I remember having a boss years ago who seemed to only call me into his office when he felt I was underperforming. He would offer direct criticisms and make it clear where I was falling short. He would then send me away to figure it out. I appreciated his *challenge* but remember feeling so alone in trying to figure out how to change course. I needed more *support* from him to balance the level of challenge.

We need Kairos partners who provide support to help us stay the course and challenge us not to deviate without good reason.

TRUSTED – Our Kairos Partner should be someone we trust, someone who has our best interest in mind. They should be someone who will cheer us on, encourage us when we're struggling and challenge us when we're trying to give up. We don't need a partner who shames us in our struggles or turns a blind eye to our resignation. They should also be someone who practices a healthy dose of discretion. After all, we can't share our deepest struggles, wondering whether they'll show up on social media or in the gossip mill.

Too often I have worked with leaders who are determined to make the journey alone, convinced they can provide their own support and challenge. This might work, but more likely leaves us susceptible to our own blind spots and either being too harsh or too easy on ourselves.

In summary, let's look for partners we trust have our best interest in mind. We need someone we feel safe to share our journey with, the good and bad. Don't settle for less than someone who can handle you with a guilt-free, judgment-free and self-interest-free attitude. Look for partners who will commit to supporting, encouraging and even pushing you along the journey. We need partners who will tenderly ask, "Are you fighting for your plan?" We also need someone who can help us recognize when our plan may not be working and help us rework our plan.

RULES OF ENGAGEMENT

In any relationship it is always helpful to clarify some rules of engagement. These set the boundaries, parameters and expectations for navigating conversations and interactions. Below are helpful rules of engagement when working with a Kairos Partner to make sure we're taking 100% personal responsibility for our journey, whilst benefiting from their input.

1. Your partner might suggest a Kairos to you, but you have to own any Kairos you decide to process.
2. You have to own whatever learning comes out of a Kairos.
3. Your partner is not responsible for your plan, you are.
4. Your partner is not responsible for your execution of the plan, you are.
5. Your partner is not responsible for your growth and transformation, you are.
6. Your partner is not responsible for your willingness to put in the hard work to stay the course, you are.
7. Partnership is always first and foremost something you're willingly inviting from another, not something they should be enforcing on you. (The only caveat to this may be a boss who implements a growth plan for you. They're your boss, so give them the benefit of the doubt.)
8. Processing and responding to Kairos moments is your choice to learn and grow.

PARTNERSHIP FOR MY MARRIAGE KAIROS

After developing a plan together with my wife, I wanted to make sure I had partnership to help me through what I knew would be a challenging season. After processing through various relationships with Kandi, I settled on inviting her, my older brother, my counselor, and my business partners to help me in my Kairos journey. All of them agreed and they continue to partner me to this day.

Kandi and I will regularly process how my journey is going and she will offer feedback on how I'm being experienced within the household. My brother and I take walks together where I share with him about my marriage, how my beliefs/narratives are impacting my daily decisions and my overall emotional wellbeing. My counselor helps me process the areas of my life where I experience anxiety, stress and my temptations to escape or medicate my pain through unhealthy coping mechanisms. My business partners (both of whom are close friends) help me process how I'm operating during travel engagements and how my attitudes and behaviors are affecting my running of our business.

As humans, I believe we are wired to know others and be known by others. We operate best when connected to meaningful relationships where we partner one another on our life journeys. Having our best and worst bits exposed before others can stir feelings of shame, guilt, regret, insecurity and inadequacy. Let me remind you that your journey is not to be compared with other people's journey. Everyone is messed up to some degree, but only you can choose to become a better version of yourself! Therefore, put a premium on finding good partners who will partner you on your journey.

PARTNERSHIP EXERCISE

Given the plan(s) you made in the previous chapter, write down some names of people you think would be trustworthy partners to provide support and challenge for your journey.

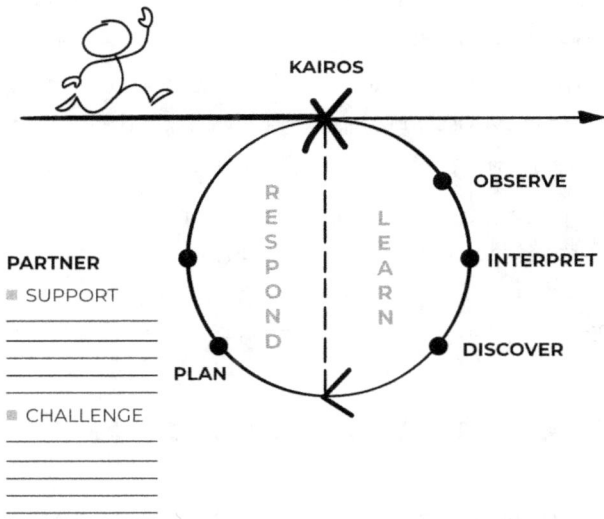

TIPS FOR PRACTICING PARTNERSHIP

- Invite your partner into your Kairos as soon as possible. They can help you sift through observations, interpretations and distill the learning/takeaways available.
- Double-check with your partner that your plan is both concrete and calendarized.
- Set a time (or regular times) when you can reflect with a friend to share how your plan is going.

- Don't be afraid for fresh Kairos moments to emerge as you process how your plan is going. Sometimes it's as we cultivate our learning through plans that we discover deeper things rising to the surface.
  - If this happens, treat the new Kairos as separate and take it around the Kairos Circle with the intent of learning something fresh.
  - What you learn may coincide with the original Kairos or may reveal something entirely new. Either way, you only win when you're learning.
- If a current partner is proving unhelpful, you can ask that partner for the specific help you're looking for in order to recalibrate the relationship. And sometimes we need to find new partners if the relationship is proving unhelpful.

PARTNER – REFLECTIVE QUESTIONS

1. Can you identify 2-3 people in your life who you trust to partner with you in processing Kairos moments to mine out the learning, plan for transformation and fight for your plans? Write those names down.
2. Think back to a time when someone partnered you well in the past through a growth journey. Keeping the Kairos Circle in mind:
3. What did they do that was helpful?
4. Did they do anything you felt was unhelpful?
5. How would you have done it differently?

10

PRACTICE

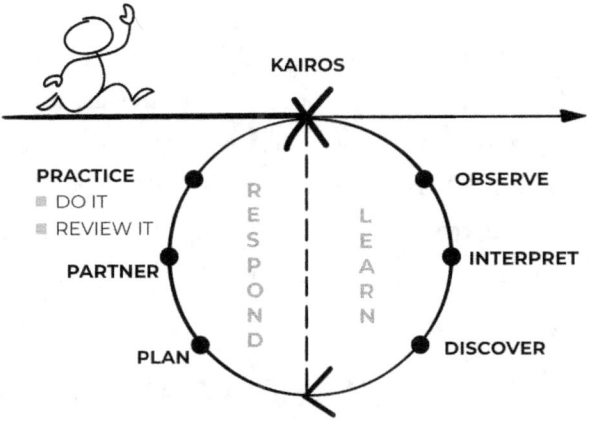

Our goal in processing every Kairos moment is to become a better version of ourselves, to put the best version of ourselves back in the driver's seat. I believe *practice makes better*, not necessarily perfect! Perfection isn't our goal, but transformation is. In this way we can ensure our impact and influence in the world is in the best interest of all parties involved. And that's how we define great leadership!

Here's a slogan many agree is spot on: JUST DO IT! This is the famous tagline that accompanied many of Nike's first television commercials and advertising campaigns in the late 80s. And it still works. Why? Thought at first to be superfluous and ineffective, it proved to hit people at a deep, visceral level. Deep down, each of us understands the life changes we seek are the result of proactive decisions and gritty follow through. We all know, no matter how much we resist it, that personal transformation requires hard work. We've gotta do the work! In order to bring any learning and plan to fruition requires we adopt the same mantra and *just do it!*

Transformation comes from a dogged commitment to practicing the plans we've decided upon until we see the desired outcomes. Growth is a process, not an event. In the same way that my wife's vegetables do not sprout overnight, our own journey toward becoming a better version of ourselves is a process that only yields results over time. Let's keep it simple - practicing any plan for sustainable success requires we Do It and Review It.

Transformation comes from a dogged commitment to practicing the plans we've decided upon until we see the desired outcomes.

DO IT – THE POWER OF PREDICTABLE PATTERNS

Often times we process Kairos moments for an immediate solution to an immediate problem, but like we talked about earlier, many of our plans will reflect ongoing changes we're looking to make to our attitudes and behaviors. It is therefore helpful to understand the power of engaging what we call predictable patterns.

Predictable patterns are any plans we make that are ongoing and require regular practice. A workout routine, regular times of meditation, weekly date nights with our significant other, consistent goal setting, and regular employee reviews are all examples of predictable patterns. These types of patterns have the best chance of cultivating long-term change. In the same way that we don't expect to get fit from one trip to the gym, a strained relationship with a coworker may require some predictable patterns of engagement and trust-building to encourage a sustainably productive relationship.

Developing any new skill or cultivating a new attitude requires predictable patterns to help us practice what we want to develop. This is the way we grew as children, and guess what—it's still the same way we grow as adults!

Let me share with you a few of the predictable patterns that have greatly helped me become a better version of myself:

1. JOURNALING - In my early 20s, my older brother introduced me to the discipline of journaling. At first I thought it was a bit narcissistic, putting my thoughts down on paper for no one to read. With my brother's partnership, I committed to this predictable pattern and have discovered many benefits. Once I stumbled upon the principles of the Kairos Circle, I realized journaling was the space I needed to ensure I was squeezing the learning from significant life experiences.

2. DATING MY CHILDREN - I have traveled quite a bit through my career, even when my children were younger. This often left me anxious about my time with them. A former mentor reminded me that consistent quality time is often more important than quantity of time. I committed to taking my kids out each week beginning when they were six and four years old. They're now twenty and eighteen, I still date them regularly and our relationship is stronger than I could have ever imagined.

3. APOLOGIZING - By far the least sexy predictable pattern I committed to years ago, but it's also been, by far, one of the most fruitful. I realized a long time ago that apologizing when I've stepped on someone's toes requires very little from me but does miracles for my relationships. I regularly ask those in my community whether I have done anything to offend them and then simply apologize. Sometimes it requires a conversation, or a trip around the Kairos Circle, but usually leads to the strengthening of these relationships by increasing trust. The people closest to me trust that I am ready and willing to apologize and change, which minimizes the feeling of risk in conflict.

POWER OF COMPOUNDING INTEREST

Predictable patterns give us the benefit of earning compounding interest on our life investments. Instead of simply adding to your investment, compounding interest multiplies it! One journaling session, one date with my children or one apology doesn't yield a whole lot, but over time these practices result in a compounding effect. I have increased my leadership intelligence significantly over the years, compounding my wisdom, through the practice of regular journaling. I have built relationships of trust, empathy, compassion, generosity and vulnerability with my children because we have regularly shared our lives with each other during regular dates. I have earned the respect, trust and loyalty of my friends, team and clients because I have regularly practiced apologizing when I cross a line.

Simply put, predictable patterns yield exponential results!

Our lives, for better and worse, are constantly revealing the compounding effects of those attitudes and behaviors we most regularly engage. It's worth taking some time to reflect on the strongest and weakest aspects of our lives and consider the predictable patterns (or attitudes and behaviors) that are netting these results. As I shared earlier in this book, it took a big wake up call for me to realize I was accruing a lot of negative compounding interest in my marriage. Even though it required multiple trips around the Kairos Circle, I was able to identify the predictable behaviors that were breaking trust with my wife and change my investment strategy. We don't transform these situations overnight, but with persistence and a commitment to healthier predictable patterns, today my relationships are on a far better trajectory!

At this point, you may be thinking about some compounding interest in your life that feels overwhelming, shameful, embarrassing, or the like. Let me say this to you: No matter how bad it is, you may not be able to change the immediate consequences. But you'll

> **You'll thank yourself till you die for owning it, taking it around the Kairos Circle and fighting for a better version of your life.**

thank yourself till you die for owning it, taking it around the Kairos Circle and fighting for a better version of your life.

I speak as one who has spent years undoing some of the compounding interest I inherited as well as investing for a better legacy for my children and their children.

Take some time to identify both helpful and unhelpful predictable patterns affecting your life. How can you cultivate the helpful ones and change the unhelpful ones?

REVIEW IT – HOW DO WE KNOW IF WE'RE WINNING?

Progress is the measure of growth, so how do we measure whether we're making progress with our plans? First, if it's a one-time plan then we can simply ask whether we acted on our plan and process the results with our Kairos Partner. We can either celebrate the success of practicing our plan or recalibrate our plan for a different result.

If it's an ongoing plan, then we'll need to review our progress at regular intervals. It will be helpful to schedule multiple review sessions with your Kairos Partner and each time to ask these simple questions together:

1. How are you doing executing on your plan?
2. Are you seeing the desired changes, results, progress?

3. Is there anything that concerns you about your plan or progress?

4. Is there anything that is making it difficult for you to continue acting on your plan?

Remember, you always have permission to review your original learning and plan with the freedom to make any helpful changes.

THINGS TO WATCH OUT FOR

In the same way my wife has to protect her garden from unwanted pests, we will also have to ward off unwanted deterrents from our plans. Here are some of the biggest temptations that undermine our ability to see a plan through until we have experienced the full measure of growth and transformation we're looking for:

FATIGUE – We all grow tired at times of practicing things that are not yet natural for us. This is normal. Don't fret. Let your Kairos Partner encourage you and recommit yourself to your plan.

SHORTCUTS – When the road gets tough, we'll likely search out shortcuts to accomplish our desired outcomes. Perhaps I buy my wife some flowers after losing my temper, hoping the flowers are a substitute for a genuine apology. Or, maybe we choose to avoid a coworker rather than have an honest conversation about brewing tensions. Again, these are shortcuts. A shortcut I'm guilty of is buying new clothes rather than addressing the fact that I'm gaining an unhealthy amount of weight. Shortcuts may seem easier in the short run but leave us worse down the road.

BIGGER IS BETTER – Sometimes we think one *big* action will substitute for small, regular predictable patterns. Maybe your family is frustrated by how much you work and so you decide to take them on an extravagant vacation. This may feel good in the moment, but it does not actually address the real issue undermining your family relationships. Or, in an attempt to pacify a complaining client, you decide to give them an extraordinary discount, eating into your needed profit margins. Of course, a vacation or discount may be a good decision, but not when it is an attempt to circumvent conflict, solve long-term problems with short-term solutions, or avoid dealing with deeper issues at hand.

There are other reasons we may struggle to stay the course. We may lose confidence in our plan and abandon it. We might lose focus in the midst of our day-to-day busyness or fail to secure partnership and try to go it alone. We may struggle to clarify our ROI along with a concrete/calendarized plan and therefore aim in the wrong direction. It's possible we become embarrassed by our struggles to execute our plan and withdraw from our partners. In any case, it's best to pay attention to where we may struggle most in order to mitigate those unwanted pests.

As I said earlier, practice makes better, not perfect. There is no shame in struggling with your plan. We simply get back on the horse and recommit ourselves to the path that leads to a better version of ourselves. All change comes through pressure and struggle so we must be brave and stick to our commitments. For this reason, it's critical that we regularly Review our progress to ensure our plan is working for us and not against us.

PRACTICE FOR MY MARRIAGE KAIROS

DO IT

Counseling Sessions – I can't tell you how often I dreaded attending counseling sessions. Some days I was exhausted from work while other days I just didn't want to deal with my inner thoughts and emotions. Even though these sessions often left me feeling better than when I entered, I struggled to muster the courage each week to bare my soul and do the hard work.

Weekly Check-Ins with Kandi – I confess it's often times easier to be vulnerable with a counselor than with my spouse. I was afraid she might hold the things I shared against me or use my vulnerability to gain the upper hand in arguments. I often found myself having to overcome these insecurities to be open and honest with her.

Discipline of Journaling for Self-Awareness – I've been practicing journaling for over twenty years, but I still experience difficulty making time for it. Sometimes I don't like what I find myself writing down. At times I feel shame rising up as I confess certain attitudes or behaviors. I think to myself, "what if someone finds my journals and reads them? The world would know what a train wreck I really am!" Nonetheless, I have found this discipline remarkably helpful in paying attention to myself and how I'm impacting others.

REVIEW IT

I will often ask Kandi or my business partners how they or others might be experiencing me. This is a radically humbling experience because as much as I love hearing where I'm winning, I know they're going to share any concerns they may have as well. I have to remind myself that growth is forged in the furnace of brutal honesty, and the pain of growth is always worth it.

I am committed to reading back over my journal every three months with the intention of reflecting on my journey, identifying areas of growth, and celebrating where I can see progress. I know this may sound laborious to some, but I promise it will yield incredible perspective, wisdom and learning.

In a recent counseling session, my counselor shared with me she thought it a good idea to take a break from the weekly session. She reflected back to me the progress I had made, and she didn't think the weekly sessions were necessary in this next season. Of course, I was nervous that without this support system I would spiral back into the pit, but as we reviewed together my journey, I became increasingly convinced and confident I had done the work and was ready for a break from this predictable pattern.

PRACTICE EXERCISE

1. For any plans you have made, make sure they are concrete and calendarized. Don't be afraid to invite someone to double-check your work.

2. Determine how you will review the progress of your plan. Do you have a clear return on investment (ROI)? Are you getting the desired outcomes? Does anything need to change?

PRACTICE – REFLECTIVE QUESTIONS

1. What gets in your way the most when practicing the plans you've made?

2. Can you identify any predictable patterns in your life that have benefited you? How would you describe the compounding interest gained from these patterns?

3. Can you identify any predictable patterns from your life that are harmful or undermining your success? Commit to making space to take these around the Kairos Circle.

4. What do you find most helpful when you are falling off your plans to get back on track?

5. Do you have any intentional practices to Review your journey and progress? What are they and how do they serve you?

11

TRAJECTORY SHIFT = TRANSFORMATION

If we practice the Kairos Circle even half-well, we will experience a trajectory shift. First, we experience a shift of how we see and lead ourselves. This will naturally lead to seeing and engaging others more effectively. It's helpful to remember, we can only give to others what we first cultivate within ourselves.

As we cultivate our learning with practiced plans, we will find not only our behaviors shift, but also our attitudes. We cannot control our environment or even the exact outcome of a journey around the Kairos Circle, but we can determine to take the path that most likely leads to personal learning, growth and transformation.

Every Kairos we process and act on leads to a trajectory shift, first internal and then external. Even if processing a Kairos only affirms our current direction, it still reinforces our desired trajectory. I often encourage my clients that doing their best to process any Kairos moment leads to transformation. Therefore, we don't have to get caught up in practicing this tool perfectly, but we do have to practice it.

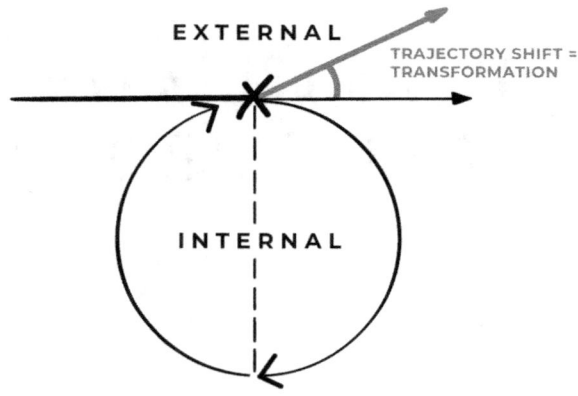

Below I want to share significant pieces of practical wisdom we often impart to clients as they put the Kairos Circle to practice for the purpose of personal and circumstantial breakthroughs.

ONE KAIROS AT A TIME

We might feel intimidated by the negative Kairos moments in our lives. Think of these negative Kairos moments like the inevitable knots that appear anytime you pull out that kite you haven't flown in a while. It seems impossible to untangle the knotted string, rendering the kite useless. My dad taught me as a child the best thing we can do is start with one knot at a time. As we loosen one knot, we may release six inches or six feet of string. We cannot always predict the result, but we do know that each Kairos we process will untangle mental, emotional and even physical areas of stress, frustration and confusion. Sometimes the string seems to untangle itself while other times require more patience and perseverance. Either way, the sure-fire way to recover clarity and confidence in how we're living our lives is to engage one Kairos at a time.

I remember speaking with a client who was really stressed about a decision they were trying to make about a new vendor that seemed like a no-brainer. The deal would significantly cut costs and increase revenues. As we processed this particular Kairos, I asked, "Is there anything else weighing on you right now? I'm having a hard time understanding why this decision is so difficult for you when it seems so obvious."

"Yes, but it has nothing to do with work," said the client. "My daughter just left for her first year at university, I've been worried sick for her and feel like a bad executive for letting my personal feelings affect my work. And I feel really silly even talking about it. I didn't hire you to be my personal shrink!"

"I understand that you want to set those boundaries," I replied, "but it sounds like this Kairos about your daughter is impacting your clarity at work, which is absolutely normal for any human being. That doesn't make you a bad executive. Let's process the Kairos about your daughter leaving for school and see how that impacts how you feel about the new vendor deal?"

She agreed. After processing for a few minutes together she was able to accept the fact that being a mother and being a CEO were both very much a part of her identity in this season and there was no need to sacrifice one on the altar of the other. Slowly, but surely, she accepted that it was ok to feel concern for her daughter, even as a high-powered executive. In the end, she made peace with the stress stemming from motherhood and this released a great deal of clarity and freedom to move froward on the new vendor deal. This is a great example of how processing one Kairos released the mental and emotional margin to tackle another Kairos more effectively!

KAIROS WITHIN A KAIROS

As we unpack a Kairos, we will often unearth more Kairos moments. For example, in my opening story, the initial Kairos was around my wife wanting a separation, but with a bit of processing, other important Kairos moments emerged. I was drinking unhealthily. I was depressed and suffering anxiety attacks. I was avoiding my household. I was gaining too much weight. These were all Kairos moments that were uncovered as I processed the initial Kairos. Each of them was very important, but I needed to tackle them one at a time.

The experience of discovering Kairos moments within a Kairos can feel deflating or overwhelming, but I assure you it is normal and to be expected. The Kairos Circle exposes deeper layers of our mental and emotional reality and will reveal deeper Kairos.' My encouragement is to recognize the new Kairos and ask yourself: Do we stick with the initial Kairos and come back to the new one later, or is the new Kairos more urgent and important to process? I can assure you there is no wrong decision here, but only determining which Kairos is a greater priority for you at that moment. There's always time to tackle the important Kairos.' I must remind myself frequently—we can only tackle one Kairos at a time.

MEASURING GROWTH

Some have doubted whether personal transformation can be measured. I say it can, and science only confirms this. Consider this—they can now chart and measure the changes in brain activity and neural pathways that reflect a change in the way someone thinks and behaves. But perhaps my favorite way of measuring transformation in leaders is anecdotal evidence. This is the information we accumulate by interviewing clients and their colleagues to determine whether attitudes and behaviors are actually shifting in the workplace.

I've worked with many companies who desire results in the form of spreadsheets, graphs and various assessments to ensure we are able to achieve the expressed deliverables. I'm not opposed to these metrics, but when dealing with human behavior, anecdotal evidence is always the best indicator of transformation. Why? Because a client can say they have changed all they want, but if the people they deal with on a regular basis don't agree, we have a major problem.

Listen carefully: the best indicator of your personal transformation is the sustained testimony of how others experience you.

The best indicator of your personal transformation is the **sustained testimony of how others experience you.**

So how do we measure personal growth and transformation? It's really no different from how we measure whether someone is learning to play the piano. Think of a piece of music like the expectations set for a performance. At first, the student must learn the various keys on the piano and how to play them in the order determined by the sheet music. As they progress, tempo and feel become a part of playing the piece more effectively. But in the end, the real question is how the piece, when played, impacts those listening.

In a similar way, we offer simple tools that act like sheet music. Our clients must first learn the basic mechanics and skills associated with healthy, effective leadership. In the beginning they are mechanical in how they operate, but with practice they become more nuanced and sophisticated in how they apply our tools. And the end goal is to determine how their new leadership skills impact others. This is measurement by anecdotal evidence and testimony.

As leadership coaches, we are concerned with:

1. sustained attitudes
2. exhibited in particular behaviors
3. over a period of time
4. that yield desired outcomes in any context

Here are simple ways we can measure the process of transformation using the Kairos Circle:

- Count how many Kairos moments an individual has processed with the Kairos Circle. (This you can put on a spreadsheet)
- Observe their ability to practice each step of the Kairos Circle, asking whether they are bypassing a step or even struggling with a step.
- Consider the value of the Learning and Takeaways mined out from any Kairos.
- Determine whether a plan is Concrete and Calendarized and whether someone is following through with their plan.
- Observe new attitudes and behaviors and determine whether they are helping or harming the environment.
- Ask whether a person is operating with sustained attitudes and/or behaviors for days, weeks or months after initiating a plan.

PROOF IN THE PUDDING

I believe we need proof in the pudding! Either the work we do to process Kairos moments leads to actual, concrete change, or we're wasting our time. For this reason, in our coaching process with clients, we are regularly reviewing and highlighting the changes in how they are operating and how others are experiencing them. *When the people around you are confirming the changes you've been fighting for, you know you're on the right track!*

Below are real stories of transformation experienced by people just like you and me. I assure you these stories are the encouragement we need to make our own way. No matter your role, title, income, or station in life, these stories tell of the powerful transformation available to each of us when we live a Kairos Lifestyle. Enjoy them. Be inspired by them. Learn from them. Most importantly, let them be fuel for your own journey.

REAL STORIES TO FUEL OUR JOURNEY

CHAD

Chad is a senior executive in a large civil construction company and is responsible for the success of their larger projects. One morning he was called to a job site to discover a feud had arisen between the project owner, the general contractor and Chad's superintendent regarding how best to proceed with a particular trench they were digging. The general contractor was upset because moving the trench would eat into his profits. Chad's superintendent was upset because he knew the current trench, which was according to the plans, would interfere with others pipes and create bigger problems down the road. The owner was upset because the debate was slowing work and delaying the finish date of this project.

When Chad arrived, he was welcomed with all three parties yelling, blaming and cursing at one another. Each was convinced the others were the problem and there was no solution in sight. Having been trained in the Kairos Circle, Chad recommended they all take a short break and then gather in the onsite office to attempt a more civil conversation. They begrudgingly agreed and reconvened thirty minutes later in the office.

Chad began by reminding everyone of their shared ROI. "We all want this job to get done. Everyone wants to do their job well and get paid. If we don't stop this arguing and figure this out together, we'll all lose." Chad proceeded to draw the Kairos Circle on a whiteboard in the office. He explained that what they were experiencing was a Kairos moment, an opportunity to learn together so they could move forward together. He walked them through each step of the tool and then asked each to share their perspective on what was going on. As they listened to one another, it was as if it was the first time they were processing the matter. Eyes and ears were opened to understand and appreciate where each was coming from. Together they decided on some key takeaways that would allow them to complete the work in a timely manner. They made a plan, partnered one another and reviewed it along the way to ensure they were on track. What before would have ended in lawsuits, instead became a powerful breakthrough for everyone involved.

I heard this story from a project manager who happened to be present for this experience. He shared how amazed he was that Chad was able to practice composure, keep his cool and lead the others into agreed partnership. When I asked him what most surprised him, he said, "In the past, Chad would have lost his shit and burned the whole project to the ground in anger. He's a different person ever since he learned this tool!"

REBECCA

Rebecca is the CEO of a competitive eyewear company; one she took over reluctantly, but was committed to growing. When our team arrived onsite for a two-day training, it became quickly apparent that the sales department was not on the same page as Rebecca. While her entire team sat through two days of hard work, her sales team had convinced her they needed to focus on sales rather than leadership and culture development. Rebecca, struggling with people-pleasing, agreed they could skip the training.

Later that evening, while sharing a meal with Rebecca and her team, I asked her why the sales team was excluded from the training. She explained their conversation, and I asked, "Rebecca, what's the weakest part of your company?" She replied, "Our sales team is struggling to secure expanding markets, but they tell me they're doing everything they can with no luck." I stared at Rebecca for a moment, remembering what I had seen at the office earlier that day, then asked, "Rebecca, it seems you're not holding these folks accountable for their sales quotas. They've been behind for months, and the only reason they give you is that 'they're trying their best with no luck?'" What I saw in the office that day was Rebecca's team working hard on developing the engine of their leadership culture, while the sales team played video games. "Rebecca, I think you're providing lots of Support for these folks and not enough Challenge! You're treating them more like spoiled children than employees."

Rebecca, with tears brewing in her eyes, acknowledged that she was being too easy on the sales team. She shared how they reminded her of her own children and that she gave them way too many chances. She learned that day that her generosity and kindness were being taken advantage of and her business would fail if she didn't learn how to balance her supportive leadership style with direct, meaningful Challenge.

I discovered some time later that Rebecca replaced most of her sales team and the company's trajectory has shifted as a result of Rebecca's trajectory shift.

JOHN

John leads a large, national distributor. He brought our coaching group in as they grew from a mom-and-pop operation to one with hundreds of employees and multiple distribution plants and operational outposts. With the ever-growing complexity of communication across so many different parts of the business, he found himself deeply frustrated with the increasing lack of communication, gossip, passive-aggressive emails and unresolved conflict.

During a coaching session, I asked John how they could resolve the dysfunctional communication practices flowing through the company that had become toxic. He laughed nervously and said, "That's why I hired you guys!" I smiled empathetically and responded, "John, the change you want in the company culture has to begin with you. Are you willing to take a hard look at the dysfunctions in your own communication to set an example for the others?" He looked down for a moment and nodded in agreement.

We began a predictable pattern of identifying those difficult communication engagements he was having so we could process them together. This would allow John to take personal responsibility for his own part in the difficulties before confronting others.

In one such conversation, John shared with me about a department leader he felt was regularly defensive about her team. He felt he couldn't bring concerns about her team to her attention for fear she would put up a wall and shut him down. He had spoken to her about his frustrations, but had determined it wasn't doing any good and resolved nothing would change. I asked John about their history and those experiences that led to this interpretation of the department leader. He shared stories that were a year old. I asked if he had recently experienced these encounters with her and he sheepishly explained it had been some time since their last altercation.

This was a great opportunity to dig a bit deeper, to understand how John had developed an interpretation of this leader that was largely rooted in old experiences. He recognized the unfairness of his perspective, that these past experiences were clouding his view of her presently, and he committed to exchanging his old lens for a new one. "Eric, to be fair, she has been quite easy to work with over the past few months, but those old memories are still so powerful." I shared how I often find myself operating in the present with unhelpful attitudes that are rooted in experiences ten (or even twenty) years old!

John not only owned his own negative bias, but also planned a conversation with this department lead to clear the air. I sat in on this meeting. I was impressed with John's humility, his courage to own the error in his perspective, and his willingness to give this team member an opportunity to share her experience. She said,

"John, you came to me a year ago and shared your difficulty with my defensiveness. I didn't like hearing it, but I saw where you were coming from. I made a commitment to behave differently so I can benefit from your perspective on my department and so you feel safe bringing your concerns to me."

I was blown away by John's willingness to develop himself despite already being a very successful leader. I was equally impressed with the department lead's willingness to receive critical feedback and fight for a healthier culture.

CORRIE

Corrie is one of the best young leaders I've had the pleasure of working with over the past few years. She was hired to be the general manager of a startup brewery on the East Coast. I was hired by the owners with the idea of establishing a powerful leadership culture from their beginning. I still remember one of the owners saying to me, "Eric, we don't want to wait until we're in a terrible mess before we call you!" I deeply appreciated this perspective and committed to helping them develop a leadership engine that would rival the incredible quality of their craft beer.

It quickly became apparent that Corrie was feeling overwhelmed by her interactions with the four owners. They were a smart and capable group, but they struggled to discern where their responsibilities ended and where Corrie's began. This led to constant communication gaps, frustrations and tensions between Corrie and the owners.

Corrie shared these Kairos moments with me in a coaching session and her sense that maybe she wasn't the right person for the job. She wasn't sure how to set boundaries with the owners and distinguish her responsibilities from theirs. We committed to processing this Kairos over the next few sessions and Corrie's trajectory shifted dramatically!

In the first session, Corrie was able to own that because she was so much younger than the owners, she felt inadequate to push back on anything they suggested. Even though she was convinced they were either missing information or had a limited perspective, she was unwilling to offer a different viewpoint to theirs. As we continued around the Kairos Circle, Corrie realized that even though she was younger, it was still her responsibility as the GM to bring the full weight of her perspective to every conversation where she might be helpful. She was helped by remembering that leadership is not dependent on age or intelligence, but maturity.

In the following session, Corrie recognized she was getting caught up in the drama brewing (pun intended) between members of the ownership team. They would often call her to advocate for their perspective on an issue, hoping Corrie would take their side against the others. The last thing Corrie wanted was to contribute to any division in the ownership team. But I noticed Corrie's frustration was largely attached to their behaviors, instead of owning her part in the drama. I asked, "Corrie, what's your part in this drama? How might you be contributing to the triangulation and dysfunction in the ownership team?" She stared back perplexed. "Eric, it's not me doing anything, it's them!" I empathized with the difficulty of her situation but reminded her the first order of business for any leader is to take 100% personal responsibility for their part in any mess. She thought for a moment and then said, "Eric, when they call me to make their case on any issue, I listen, but never push back. I should be redirecting them to talk to one another about their issues rather than dragging me into their drama." Yes! Corrie was learning a critical lesson of leadership: we can only take responsibility for *our part* in dysfunctional situations.

YOU CAN DO IT!

The stories you've just read are real accounts of leaders like yourself who have decided that a Kairos Mindset leads to far better results than living on a "wing and a prayer." Each of these leaders represent different positions, incomes, scopes of influence and weight of responsibility. However, they all speak to the real situations we find ourselves in. Whether we're leading in our homes, our workplaces, in politics or professional sports, the world needs more leaders who take responsibility for their contribution to any situation. We must offer the best version of ourselves for all parties involved. For this, we need the Kairos Circle.

REFLECTIVE QUESTIONS

1. Can you identify a personal transformation you've experienced and how it unfolded? What happened and what did you learn from it?

2. Can you identify a time when you resisted a trajectory shift and lost an opportunity for personal growth? Explain.

3. Identify one takeaway from the stories above and how you can implement that in your own journey.

PART THREE

KEY APPLICATIONS OF THE KAIROS CIRCLE

In this next section, we'll cover the five key applications of the Kairos Circle that will take our leadership and our cultures to the next level.

1. Self-Coaching
2. Coaching Others
3. Collaborative Decision-Making
4. Conflict Engagement
5. Reviewing People & Projects

12

APPLICATION #1 – SELF-COACHING

We've already covered this as the first and primary application of the Kairos Circle. Our ability to process our own Kairos moments equips us to help others process their Kairos moments. The skills we learn in taking our Kairos moments around the Circle directly translates into our ability to do the same for others. Processing our Kairos moments is a form of self-coaching, perhaps the most important skill for any leader to develop. Our ability to coach ourselves encourages personal responsibility and a proactive posture. This is also how we regain our mental, emotional and even physical sobriety so that we can give the best version of ourselves to any situation.

Things to remember about self-coaching using the Kairos Circle:

- Process one Kairos at a time.
- Do your best to observe and interpret, but make sure to invite a trusted friend to help you verify your thoughts and partner you in the discovery process.

- There's no rush to get around the Kairos Circle, but don't give yourself permission to put an important Kairos on the back burner. Unprocessed Kairos moments have a way of coming back to hurt us down the road.

- No matter how much you think you can go life alone, you stand a far better chance of experiencing personal growth and transformation when you invite trusted friends to partner you in the journey.

- Remember, we can only lead others to the degree we lead ourselves. Processing your own Kairos moments gives you the integrity to help others do the same.

- Remember, every experience is just another Kairos, an opportunity to learn and grow.

PRACTICE SELF-COACHING

WHAT IS MY KAIROS?

- MY PRACTICE?
- MY PARTNER?
- MY PLAN?
- MY OBSERVATIONS?
- MY INTERPRETATIONS?
- MY DISCOVERIES?

RESPOND | LEARN

You'll notice when self-coaching, the emphasis is on *my* Kairos. This helps us practice personal responsibility by owning what's impacting us. Our experiences may impact us, but how we respond is entirely up to us. Therefore, self-coaching is marked by *my* journey around the Circle.

Below is a simple reminder to ask the appropriate questions for each step of the Circle while maintaining a posture of personal ownership for our Kairos:

(What follows is a simple outline (or cheat sheet) to remind you of the key questions to ask yourself when processing a Kairos moment.)

Kairos: What is MY Kairos?

Observe: What are MY observations?
- What are my facts?
- What are my feelings?

Interpret: What are MY interpretations?
- How am I making sense of this Kairos experience?
- Why am I being impacted this way?

Discover: What are MY discoveries?
- What am I learning about myself and others?
- What are my takeaways from this experience?

Plan: What is MY plan?
- What is my concrete and calendarized response to what I'm learning?

Partner: Who is MY partner?
- Who will provide the support and challenge I need to execute my plan?

Practice: What is MY practice?
- How will I measure whether my plan is working?
- How often will I review my plan to ensure I'm making progress?

13

APPLICATION #2 – COACHING OTHERS

As we practice processing our own Kairos moments, we'll develop greater confidence to help others do the same. Partnering with others in their Kairos moments is at the core of our leadership responsibility to develop others. One of the key ways we develop others is to partner them in identifying and processing their Kairos moments with the intent to learn and grow.

In coaching others, we simply turn the focus from *my* Kairos to *your* Kairos. Let's look at how to simply and effectively help others process their Kairos moments.

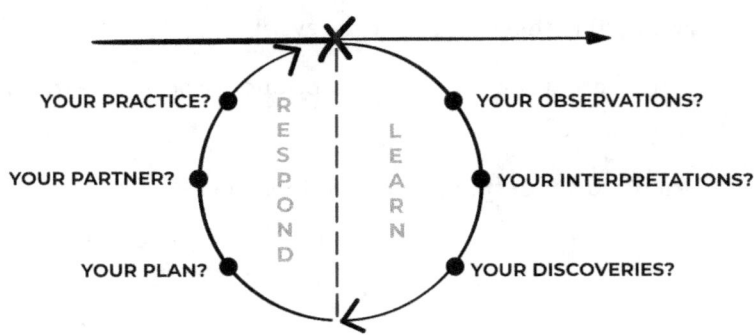

KAIROS – First, we want to help others identify the most relevant Kairos moments their experiencing. Below are some helpful questions to solicit Kairos moments from others:

- What most grabbed your attention?
- What's most sticking out to you?
- Where are you experiencing strong feelings/sensations?
- Is there anything someone else has brought to your attention?
- What's going well? What's not going well?
- What's most weighing on you?

OBSERVE – Ask them to unpack their experience, story or event related to the Kairos. To do this, ask them The Who, What, Where, When, and How questions.

- What happened?
- Who was involved?
- When did this happen?
- What did the other parties say/do?
- What did others say about the event?
- What are your strongest emotions associated with the experience?
- How did you respond in this Kairos moment?

INTERPRET – Ask them how they're making sense of their experience and feelings.

- Why do you think things turned out this way?
- How do you make sense of this experience?
- What is the story you're telling yourself?
- Could you see this experience from an alternative perspective?
- Is your narrative giving yourself/others the benefit of the doubt?
- Does your story reveal any hidden biases/prejudices toward yourself/others?

DISCOVER – Ask them what they might be learning from this Kairos.

- What are you learning about yourself or others through this Kairos?
- Is there a better version of yourself that needs to be expressed here?
- Is there a yes or no that needs to be expressed (boundaries)?
- Is there a lie you're believing that needs to be exchanged for an empowering truth?
- What are your takeaways from this Kairos?
- What insights and wisdom are you taking away?

PLAN – Ask them how they might best respond to what they're learning.

- How can you practically respond to what you're learning?
- What is a concrete and calendarized plan to help you practice what you're learning?
- What plan will help you or others operate as an asset to the environment?
- What might get in the way of your plan?

PARTNER – Ask them who they trust who would be willing to partner them in their plan.

- Who do you trust to share your learning and plan with?
- When are you going to review your process/progress with your partner?
- How can you coach yourself and receive encouragement when you feel discouraged?
- What might make it difficult to be totally honest with your partner?

PRACTICE – Ask them how they'll know whether practicing their plan is working.

- Are you clear about how you're going to practice your plan?
- What might inhibit your practice?
- What changes do you expect to see as a result of your practice?
- How will you measure and review your progress?

14

APPLICATION #3 – COLLABORATIVE DECISION-MAKING

The Kairos Circle will help us lead through any problem-solving or decision-making process in a team context. Too often we sit in meetings where only a few people actually get to contribute to a decision. A good rule is: if you don't want people to contribute to a decision, don't invite them to the meeting.

Those who are invited into a decision-making process will feel seen, heard and valued when we create intentional space for everyone's contribution. Of course, we don't want a free-for-all environment, but rather a facilitated space where we get to harness the collective genius of the group. The Kairos Circle gives us a simple, effective framework to do just that!

In this application we'll shift from *my* or *your* Kairos to *our* Kairos.

WHAT WE CAN EXPECT FROM THIS PROCESS

1. We gain collective *buy-in,* as everyone feels included and valued in the process, even if the leader has to make a final decision.

2. We learn *from* one another and *about* one another.

3. We harness the collective perspective, insight and problem-solving intelligence to discover the best possible solution.

4. We build unity and trust.

5. We have an opportunity to shift the collective narrative toward the best version of the group.

6. We experience collective transformation through the process of learning and growing together.

WHAT IS OUR KAIROS?

- OUR PRACTICE?
- OUR PARTNER?
- OUR PLAN?

RESPOND | LEARN

- OUR OBSERVATIONS?
- OUR INTERPRETATIONS?
- OUR DISCOVERIES?

OUR KAIROS – It's important to rally around a clear, agreed upon Kairos.

- What's most grabbing our attention?
- What first alerted us to this Kairos?

OBSERVE – Ask the group to take turns sharing their observations.

- What are we seeing?
- What data points are we potentially missing?
- What are we feeling about this Kairos?
- How might our emotions cloud our judgment?

INTERPRET – Ask the group to take turns sharing how they're understanding or making sense of this Kairos.

- How are we understanding this Kairos?
- What are the stories/narratives we're interpreting this Kairos through?
- What biases/prejudices/assumptions are we carrying into this decision?
- Is there anything we might not understand clearly?
- How might our feelings impact how we see this problem/decision?

DISCOVER – Ask the group to take turns sharing their insights, takeaways, learnings.

- What are we learning from all we've processed?
- What's the best possible outcome for this situation?
- What is the possible win-win solution for all parties involved?
- What might it look like for us to move forward together?
- What are our takeaways?
- What wisdom can we capture from this conversation?

PLAN – Ask the group to take turns sharing possible plans for moving forward.

- How might we best respond to this Kairos?
- What practical plans will help us address the issues we've discovered in ways that honor our discoveries?
- Is our plan concrete and calendarized?

PARTNER – Ask the group to take turns sharing who might be most helpful to provide the necessary support and challenge to ensure our plan is executed well.

PRACTICE – Ask the group to take turns sharing what metrics and feedback will help them determine whether their plan is achieving the desired outcomes. Remember, we gotta do it and review it!

APPLICATION #4 – CONFLICT ENGAGEMENT

This may be the application most dreaded by our clients, and for obvious reasons. Who wakes up in the morning excited to engage conflict? With as much practice as I have in this area, I still find myself battling mild feelings of anxiety when entering conflict conversations. Let me offer us a simple perspective that will transform the way we approach conflict. First, conflict is an inevitable human experience. To accomplish anything great in the world we have to partner with others, which will probably yield conflict at some point. Second, instead of dreading or avoiding conflict, what if we could learn to see it for what it is – an opportunity to learn and grow!

Instead of dreading or avoiding conflict, what if we could learn to see it for what it is – an opportunity to learn and grow!

Conflict is neutral, which is to say it is simply revealing a difference of perspectives or opinions. And we only think the way we do today because we've been willing to change our minds over the years. Every conflict is an opportunity to see something clearer, gain new and empowering perspective or confirm our current views. We see conflict as negative because of painful experiences in our past where it was not handled well and led to negative outcomes. Therefore, our goal here is to offer a simple, highly effective pathway to engage conflict that leads to the best interest for all parties involved.

Conflict can trigger our human defense mechanisms - fight, flight or freeze. Some people will try to overpower conflict to get their way, while others will withdraw or become passive aggressive. I find this is because many approach conflict as a *win-lose ultimatum*. The Kairos Circle empowers us to flip this script and see conflict as a *win-win proposition*. Conflict is an opportunity to learn about ourselves and others, to consider differing viewpoints and discover the best possible way forward. Therefore, we call any conflict a Conflict Kairos.

I'm not saying we have to agree with one another's perspectives to win, but we do have to remember that Conflict Kairos is primarily an opportunity to forge greater trust, respect and appreciation between both parties. A *win-lose* mindset will break relationship because it elevates the value of one person over the other, where a *win-win* approach recognizes the partnership is more valuable than who's right or wrong.

Every Conflict Kairos is an opportunity to learn and grow together. Every Conflict Kairos is an opportunity for *win-win* solutions. In part, we need to disrupt our old narratives that tell us conflict is unsafe, as well as embrace a new narrative of conflict that gives us hope for shared learning and a collaborative way forward.

> As we step into the practical application for conflict engagement, let me encourage you to always process your Conflict Kairos at a personal level first. This will equip you to enter the conflict conversation with another person from a posture of 100% personal responsibility. Having processed your perspective and emotions apart from the other party will ensure you enter the conversation with greater clarity, composure and a preparedness to learn. Self-awareness and self-leadership are the best preparations before entering a conflict conversation.

Now, we'll learn together a step-by-step process for utilizing the Kairos Circle to help us negotiate any conflict with another party.

In this application you'll notice we are integrating "My Kairos" and "Your Kairos", which leads to "Our Kairos." Pay careful attention to this shift as it has a significant impact on our experiences of conflict engagement. I'll take you step-by-step through these simple movements.

STEP #1 – MY KAIROS, OBSERVATIONS & INTERPRETATIONS

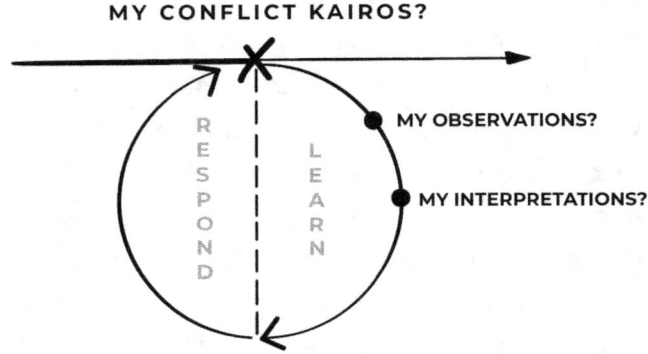

MY KAIROS – Begin by sharing "My Kairos" with the other party.

- This might sound like, "Thanks for taking some time to process something that has been on my mind. I'd like to share with you something that caught my attention from our last engagement together."

- Clarify the rules of engagement: "Once I've shared my experience and interpretation, I'd like to give you an opportunity to clarify and offer your own perspective. I'd like this to be a learning opportunity for both of us. In the end, I'd like to find a way to move forward with a win-win solution."

- If you have sufficiently processed your own Kairos, you will be better equipped to engage a Conflict Kairos with clarity of mind, emotion and body.

MY OBSERVATIONS

- Do your best to share your experience from your perspective. It's important to include both your understanding of the facts of the event and the feelings that came up for you.
- Use language like:
    - "I saw"
    - "I heard"
    - "I felt"
- Avoid language like:
    - "You did"
    - "You said"
    - "You made me feel"

MY INTERPRETATIONS

- It's vital to continue sharing with language that clearly communicates this is your perspective on what happened.
- By sharing in this way, it will be easier for the other party not to grow defensive and hear what you're sharing.
- It's also important for us to continue in the mode of taking 100% personal responsibility for the fact that this is "My Kairos."
- Use language like:
    - "Let me share with you how I read the situation…"
    - "I'd like to explain how I am making sense of what I experienced…"

o "This is my interpretation of the events that transpired…"

- Avoid any statements that begin with "You…"
- Avoid any statements that are conclusive, condemning or judging.
- Remind the other party you are only sharing from your perspective and will give them a moment to clarify and share their perspective.

Now, it's time to invite the other party to share their observations and interpretations. This might be difficult since their views may be different to ours, however it's essential to listen well and seek to learn from their perspective and have them feel seen, heard and valued in the relationship.

STEP #2 – YOUR OBSERVATIONS & INTERPRETATIONS

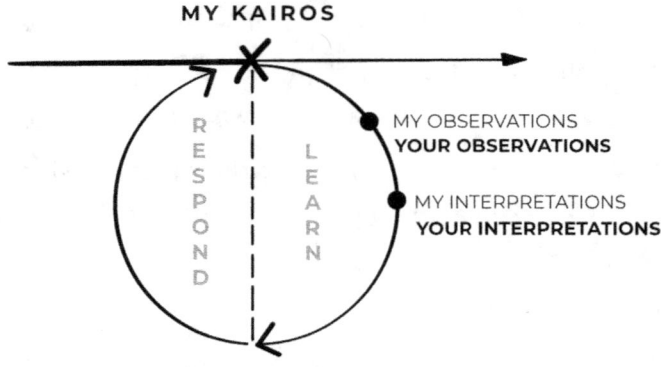

YOUR OBSERVATIONS

- Invite the other party to share what they experienced, their facts and feelings.

- Be sure to ask clarifying questions without judgment.

- It may be helpful to ask questions that begin with "who," "what," "where," and "when." For example:

  o Who was involved?

  o What happened from your perspective? What did you feel?

  o Where did this happen?

  o When did this happen?

YOUR INTERPRETATIONS

- Invite the other party to share how they understood or made sense of the Kairos experience.

- We have to remember that our conflict is exactly that—our conflict. This means we've interpreted the conflict from our point of view. We must recognize that our perspective could be flawed, misinformed or unhelpfully skewed.

- Now we give the other party an opportunity to enlighten our perspective, to help us learn from alternative views and interpretations.

- We can make two very important inquiries that will leave the other party feeling seen and heard:

  o "What am I missing?"

- o "Help me understand…"
- By asking the questions above, we are acknowledging there may be information or perspective that could correct or enhance our view. This empowers the other party to feel they are participating in the conversation, rather than just being spoken at.
- Humility on our part is key when engaging conflict. We cannot control the other party, but we can control our own attitudes and behaviors in any engagement, no matter how difficult.

Now, it's time to shift to "Our Kairos." After both parties feel seen, heard and valued, it's time to discover what we're learning from the conversation, identify any takeaways and to begin imagining a way forward that is in both parties' interest.

STEP #3 – OUR DISCOVERIES, PLAN, PARTNERS & PRACTICE

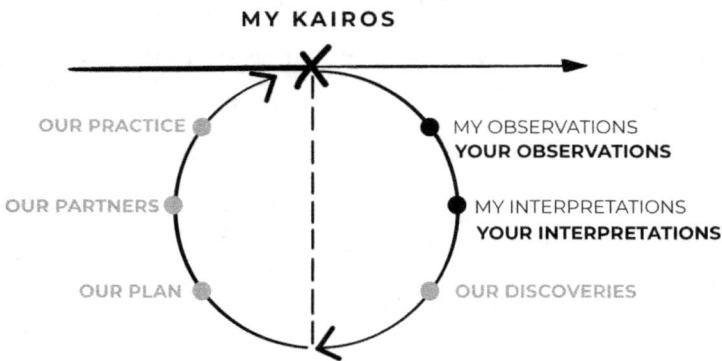

STEP#3 - OUR KAIROS

OUR DISCOVERIES

- What are we learning about ourselves, and others involved?
- What changes do I (or we) need to make to move forward?
- What takeaways may help us partner more effectively?
- What do we think is the best outcome for all parties involved?

CONFLICT ENGAGEMENT AMIDST AUTHORITY STRUCTURES

When dealing with conflict, the other party's contribution may or may not change your perspective. It's important to ask clarifying questions about anything they share. The temptation is to defend our point of view, but this will only ensure a win-lose outcome. Remember, the purpose of engaging conflict is to learn together and move forward together with a win-win solution.

The ideal outcome is shared understanding, appreciation, learning and the discovery of a way forward. But we all know that conflict doesn't always move in this direction.

How do we respond when it seems there is no pathway to reconciliation available?

If you are the authority figure:

- I recommend double-checking your perspective with another, but if you still feel the other party is in the wrong, this may be an opportunity to give the other party a decision:
  - They do their best to align their attitudes and behaviors with what we believe is in the best interest of all parties involved, or

- o They decide to seek another context in which they can pursue what they believe is better.
- And sometimes we realize it's time to part ways with the other party.

If you are dealing with an authority figure:

- It may be worth asking if another authority figure can mediate.
- If this isn't available or doesn't work, you may have a decision to make about whether it's the right context for you to continue in.

If you are dealing with a peer:

- Invite a trusted third party to mediate toward a win-win solution.
- If this isn't available or doesn't work, then you may have a decision to make about continuing in this shared context.

It's important to remember that not all conflict ends the way we hope. With unreconciled conflict we will have to decide whether we can agree to disagree and continue in the relationship, or whether a parting of ways is necessary.

WARNING: From my perspective, to continue in any relationship (boss, client, coworker, significant other) where unresolved conflict leads to toxicity, it is a lose-lose scenario. Too many people tolerate toxicity in relationships for fear of the loss of a job, friendship, partnership or opportunity. Your personal health and wellbeing aren't worth any amount of money, position or partnership. It's time to set healthy boundaries and discover your better future!

OUR PLAN

If both parties have been able to see eye-to-eye, it's time to develop a plan to respond to the shared learning.

- Remember to make a plan that honors the takeaways.
- Every plan must be concrete and calendarized.
- Every plan must reflect a win-win solution.
- No matter the dynamic of relationship, it is important that both parties agree on the plan, otherwise it's unlikely it will serve its purpose.

OUR PARTNERS

Determine whether it would be helpful to find outside partnership for support and challenge in executing the plan. This is especially important when there has been tension in resolving the conflict. If not, then both parties may serve as partners for the agreed-upon plan.

OUR PRACTICE

Discuss with the other party how you will determine together whether the plan is achieving its desired outcome.

- Remember, it's always ok to review how the plan is going and if needed, recalibrate the plan to ensure it is helpful.
- It may be valuable to include outside partners in reviewing how the plan is going, to have some objective perspective in both parties' favor. This is especially true when there is an imbalance of power between the two parties.

16

APPLICATION #5 – REVIEWING PEOPLE & PROJECTS

We're all familiar with various review processes implemented by leaders and organizations. Some are quarterly reviews, while others may happen annually. Mid-project or post-project reviews sometimes happen as well.

The often-stated purpose of these review meetings is to learn from our journey and make the necessary adjustments for growth and development. Sadly, we have discovered from working with many organizations that this purpose is rarely achieved. Why? The problem we find is not with the stated purpose, but with the methodology to achieve said purpose. When we ask leaders their methodology, we're often met with blank stares. "What do you mean our methodology?" Or, "I use reviews to simply let people know whether they're failing or succeeding." Another popular response is, "Reviews are how we keep people in check. If they know they are being reviewed at some point in the future, they'll work harder today."

Again, the problem is found when there is a gap between the method and purpose. Most leaders do not have an intentional methodology for review that will achieve the desired outcome of *learning* and *growth*.

The best methodology for reviewing a person's performance, project, goals, etc. is to identify and process Kairos moments. Why? Because the purpose of the tool is to create space for learning and development. The discipline of reviewing anything is to identify the key Kairos moments, which give us access to learning and opportunity to celebrate what's going well, along with course-correction.

REVIEW TIPS

As you review with an individual or team, you're simply looking for the Kairos moments that emerge. They will reveal the greatest opportunities for learning, growth and development.

To solicit the relevant Kairos moments, we can ask these questions:

- What were the things that most caught your attention during this project?
- What went well and what didn't go well from your perspective?
- Is there anything you think we could have done differently?
- Was there anything that surprised you?
- What do you think you did well? Where could you have performed more effectively?

- Do you think you/we were successful? Why?
- If we were going to do this again, what might you change?

Once we have solicited Kairos moments, we can now pick the most relevant ones to review using the Kairos Circle.

FREQUENCY & FORMALITY

Another way of talking about a review process is a feedback loop. A feedback loop can be either formal or informal and have a short or long frequency. A formal feedback loop may look like a scheduled meeting to identify and process the relevant Kairos moments. An informal feedback loop may look like asking the other person(s) how they, a project or particular goals are coming along while riding the elevator together, sharing a lunch, or while on the golf course. Of course, we need to be careful we don't accidentally hijack the other party by getting too serious in a context that is meant to be relaxing or fun.

Frequency is particularly important to consider when it comes to reviewing individual or team performance. As humans, we thrive in any environment that provides a short feedback loop. The further removed we are from an experience, the more difficult it becomes to mine the learning available—not impossible, but more difficult.

The frequency of the feedback loop should reflect the particular needs of the individual or team. A 10-minute team standup review at the beginning or end of a day can help us identify problems more readily and stay on the same page. At other times, this frequency will be unhelpful and cause everyone to feel their time is being wasted. Some projects require more regular communication and connection between parties involved, while others may not. A weekly or even bi-weekly review may be helpful, but the most important thing is discerning what frequency serves the team best.

Some individuals thrive on regular, informal reviews, where you might stop by their desk or chat them up about how they're doing on the way to a restaurant. Others will thrive by knowing exactly when and how they can expect to discuss performance, projects and goals.

Finding the right frequency and balance between formal/informal reviews can take some experimentation, but guess what? Every time you slow down to reflect on your reviews, simply identify the relevant Kairos moments and use the Kairos Circle to learn, grow and develop a more effective review strategy. It can also be helpful to invite those you review to give feedback in this process. Just remember, these touch points should serve your team, not the other way around.

AFTERWORD

PERSONAL RESPONSIBILITY – IT'S WORTH IT!

In my experience, leaders plateau for lack of a simple, clear way of addressing their own leadership deficiencies. We can only lead others to the degree we can lead ourselves. This being said, there is no substitute for putting in the hard work of practicing self-awareness and self-leadership. This is the not-so-sexy, behind-the-scenes, unheralded pathway to becoming a better version of yourself.

The best leaders I work with recognize it has to start with them, and that they can't ask others to do what they have not been willing to do. No matter how successful we become, there is always more work we can do on ourselves. So don't cheat yourself. Do the work. Put this tool into practice on a regular basis and watch your leadership and the culture around you shift in unimaginable ways.

Let's remember, we can only give to others what we have first cultivated within ourselves. All the work we do on ourselves radically transforms our ability to lead and serve others in the same ways. Your effort will never be wasted, even if it may be challenging.

You are the leader the world around you needs. We can't be perfect today, but we can strive to give others a better version of ourselves each and every day. Join us in this pursuit. It's worth it!

MY MARRIAGE

Choosing the opening story of my wife confronting me with a possible separation as the overarching narrative, was the greatest challenge in writing this book. It's never fun to expose your inadequacies and failures for all to read or hear about. However, years ago, I committed to leading others out of the overflow of my own journey. I choose to speak and write from a place of honesty, vulnerability and transparency. Why? I hope my example will give you courage to do the same.

In life and leadership, we often find ourselves confronted with very challenging experiences and decisions. We cannot afford to fly by the seat of our pants, or wing our responses. We need a simple and clear process we can use for every Kairos moment that will give us the best chance for desirable trajectories.

Currently, my wife and I continue on the journey of identifying and processing those Kairos moments that are impacting our marriage and family. Each Kairos is an opportunity for me to take a look beneath the hood of my own life and own where I'm operating poorly. We also celebrate the positive Kairos moments - those experiences that prove new attitudes and behaviors are taking root through healthier predictable patterns.

Kandi stays married to me, not because I have figured it all out, but because I'm committed to a Kairos mindset. Every conversation, every decision and every experience we share together is just another Kairos, an opportunity to learn and grow together. The best thing I can give to those around me is a commitment to my own personal transformation. And for this reason, I'm convinced

I'll be processing Kairos moments till the day I die. Thankfully, I have the best Kairos processing partner in my amazing wife!

Whether in our personal relationships, at work, or in everyday interactions with other people, we owe it to ourselves and others to engage life with a certain degree of intentionality. My hope is that the Kairos Circle will equip and empower you to live your life intentionally. I look forward to hearing your stories of breakthrough and success as you put the the Kairos Circle to work to make all of life happen for you, rather than to you! After all, this is your superpower.

After all, this is your **superpower.**

APPENDIX

KAIROS TEMPLATES

Kairos Circle Template

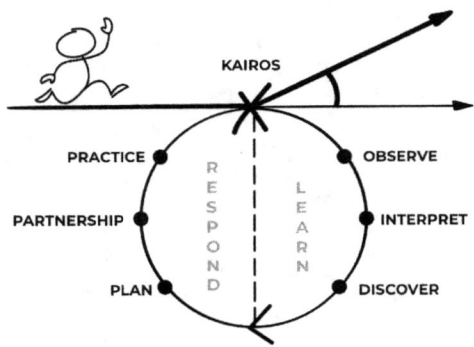

KAIROS (What most grabbed your attention?)

OBSERVE (Facts & Feelings?)

APPENDIX: KAIROS CIRCLE TEMPLATE | 193

INTERPRET (Why did this happen? How do you make sense of it?)

DISCOVER (What are you learning? What are your takeaways?)

PLAN (Concrete & Calendarized?)

PARTNER (Who will you invite to support and challenge you on your journey?)

PRACTICE (Do it & Review it)

Kairos Circle Template

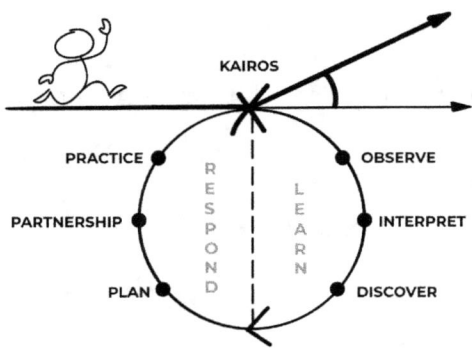

KAIROS (What most grabbed your attention?)

OBSERVE (Facts & Feelings?)

APPENDIX: KAIROS CIRCLE TEMPLATE | **195**

INTERPRET (Why did this happen? How do you make sense of it?)

DISCOVER (What are you learning? What are your takeaways?)

PLAN (Concrete & Calendarized?)

PARTNER (Who will you invite to support and challenge you on your journey?)

PRACTICE (Do it & Review it)

Kairos Circle Template

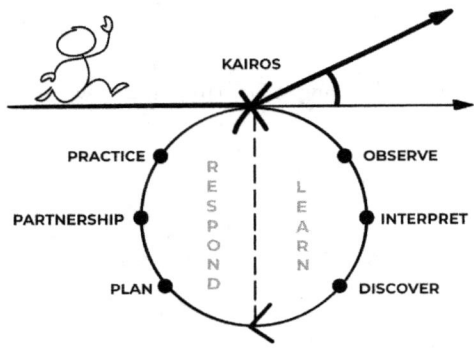

KAIROS (What most grabbed your attention?)

OBSERVE (Facts & Feelings?)

APPENDIX: KAIROS CIRCLE TEMPLATE | 197

INTERPRET (Why did this happen? How do you make sense of it?)

DISCOVER (What are you learning? What are your takeaways?)

PLAN (Concrete & Calendarized?)

PARTNER (Who will you invite to support and challenge you on your journey?)

PRACTICE (Do it & Review it)

www.ingramcontent.com/pod-product-compliance
Lightning Source LLC
Chambersburg PA
CBHW071239070526
44583CB00017B/2253